PMI-RMP
EXAM CONTENT
OUTLINE

2023

A Comprehensive Study Guide
for the PMI Risk Management
Professional Certification

British Library cataloguing in the publication data is available.

ISBN: 978-1-916720-18-3

This book is dedicated to you — the aspiring risk management professionals, the curious learners, and the dedicated practitioners who strive every day to make informed decisions in the face of uncertainty.

TABLE OF CONTENTS

Alexander Stratton

2

Introduction

Welcome to "PMI-RMP Exam Content Outline: A Comprehensive Study Guide for the PMI Risk Management Professional Certification," an essential resource for those aspiring to become certified Risk Management Professionals through the Project Management Institute (PMI). This guide is meticulously crafted to align with the latest PMI standards and the revered PMBOK Guide, ensuring you receive the most up-to-date and relevant information in the field of project risk management.

Our journey through this book will take you deep into the heart of the PMI-RMP exam, dissecting each domain, task, and enabler that forms the backbone of the exam content outline. We understand that the path to certification is not just about passing an exam; it's about developing a robust understanding of risk management principles and their practical application in real-world scenarios. This guide serves as your compass in navigating through the complexities of risk management, providing clear, concise, and comprehensive coverage of all necessary topics.

Each section of this book is designed to enhance your understanding of the critical domains of project risk management. We delve into the specific tasks associated with each domain, offering illustrative examples and real-life scenarios that bring these concepts to life. These practical insights are not only instrumental in helping you clear the PMI-RMP exam but also invaluable in shaping your approach to managing risks in diverse project environments.

Moreover, this guide acknowledges the dynamic nature of risk management and the need for a proactive approach in identifying, analyzing, and responding to risks. As such, we integrate the latest trends, tools, and techniques in risk management. ensuring you are equipped with contemporary knowledge and skills.

Whether you are a seasoned project manager or new to the field of risk management, this guide is tailored to meet your learning needs. It paves the way for a successful journey towards achieving PMI-RMP certification, bolstering your confidence and competence as a professional in this ever-evolving discipline.

Embark on this educational adventure with us, and let's unlock the door to excellence in project risk management together.

DOMAIN I
RISK STRATEGY
AND PLANNING

Task 1 Perform a preliminary document analysis

COMPILATION AND ANALYSIS OF PRELIMINARY DOCUMENTS

In the context of risk strategy and planning, particularly under Task 1 of Domain I, "Gather and Review Documents" is a critical step in the initial phase of risk management. This task forms the foundation for identifying and analyzing potential risks in a project. The documents you review at this stage can significantly influence the effectiveness of the entire risk management process. Let's delve into the examples of preliminary documents to review:

1. **Industry Benchmarks**: These are critical for understanding the standard practices and performance metrics within your industry. They provide a comparative basis to evaluate your project's potential risks and opportunities. Industry benchmarks may include data on project success rates, common risk factors in similar projects, and standard response strategies.

2. **Previous Lessons Learned**: Reviewing lessons learned from past projects within your organization can offer invaluable insights. This documentation often includes analyses of what worked well and what

didn't, helping you anticipate and mitigate similar risks in your current project. It's a rich source of practical, experiential knowledge.

3. **Historical Data**: Historical project data is crucial for risk identification. This includes project timelines, budget records, quality reports, and any instances of scope changes. Analyzing this data can help you identify patterns and trends that may pose risks to your current project.

4. **Sources of Information**: It's essential to identify and evaluate the sources of your benchmark, lessons learned, and historical data. Assessing the reliability and relevance of these sources ensures that your risk assessment is based on accurate and pertinent information. Sources might include internal company records, industry publications, and databases, or consultations with experts in the field.

In summary, the preliminary document analysis in risk management involves a comprehensive review of industry benchmarks, previous lessons learned, and historical data, along with a critical evaluation of their sources. This initial analysis sets the stage for effective risk identification and management throughout the project lifecycle.

ASSIGNMENT OF PRELIMINARY DOCUMENT ANALYSIS RESPONSIBILITIES

Determining and assigning responsibility for the preliminary document analysis is a crucial step in the risk management process. This task involves identifying the key personnel who will be responsible for gathering, reviewing, and analyzing the various documents that form the basis for risk identification. Let's explore the roles that might be involved:

1. **Project Manager**: The project manager often plays a central role in preliminary document analysis. They have a comprehensive understanding of the project's objectives, constraints, and requirements. The project manager is well-positioned to identify relevant historical data and lessons learned from previous projects. They can also effectively coordinate with other team members to gather necessary information.

2. **Risk Manager**: A risk manager specializes in identifying and mitigating risks. In the context of document analysis, they are pivotal in interpreting industry benchmarks, evaluating historical data, and integrating lessons learned into the current project's risk framework.

Their expertise is crucial in ensuring that the risk identification process is thorough and aligned with best practices.

3. **Financial Controller**: In projects where financial risks are significant, the financial controller's involvement in document analysis is vital. They can provide insights into financial benchmarks, previous financial performance, and budgetary implications that could impact the project. Their expertise in financial analysis ensures that economic risks are adequately identified and assessed.

4. **Collaborative Effort**: Often, the responsibility for preliminary document analysis is not limited to a single role. It can be a collaborative effort involving the project manager, risk manager, financial controller, and other key stakeholders. This collaborative approach ensures a multi-dimensional analysis of risks, leveraging the diverse expertise of different team members.

5. **Clear Assignment of Responsibilities**: Regardless of who is involved, it is imperative to clearly define and communicate the responsibilities for each role in the document analysis process. This clarity helps prevent overlaps and gaps in the risk analysis and ensures a cohesive and comprehensive approach to risk management.

In summary, determining and assigning responsibility for preliminary document analysis involves considering the unique aspects of the project and the expertise required to effectively identify risks. The roles of project manager, risk manager, and financial controller are often key, but a collaborative approach can be highly beneficial for a holistic understanding of potential risks. Clear definition and communication of responsibilities are essential for the success of this process.

IDENTIFICATION OF KEY DOCUMENTS FOR THE RISK MANAGEMENT PROCESS

Establishing relevant documents for the risk process is a critical step in the risk management strategy. This involves identifying and selecting the types of documentation that will provide valuable insights into potential risks and inform the decision-making process. The choice of documents should align with the project's scope, nature, and specific risk factors. Here are some key types of documents that are typically relevant to the risk process:

1. **Project Charter**: The project charter outlines the project's objectives, scope, stakeholders, and high-level constraints. It's a foundational document for understanding the project's baseline, against which risks can be assessed.

2. **Stakeholder Register**: This document lists all stakeholders involved in the project, their roles, interests, and potential impact on the project. Understanding stakeholders is crucial for identifying risks related to stakeholder engagement and expectations.

3. **Project Management Plan**: The project management plan includes detailed information on the project's scope, schedule, cost, quality, resources, communication, and procurement. Each component of this plan can present specific risks that need to be managed.

4. **Risk Management Policy**: This document outlines the organization's approach to risk management. It includes the methodologies, tools, and techniques to be used in risk identification, analysis, response planning, and monitoring.

5. **Risk Register**: An essential document in the risk process, the risk register is a dynamic tool that lists identified risks, their analysis, and plans for risk responses. It's regularly updated throughout the project lifecycle.

6. **Lessons Learned Repository**: This contains insights from previous projects, highlighting what worked well and what didn't. Reviewing this can help identify potential risks and effective risk response strategies.

7. **Resource Calendars**: These provide information on resource availability, which is critical in identifying risks related to resource constraints.

8. **Financial Documents**: Budget estimates, cash flow projections, and cost management plans are vital for understanding financial risks.

9. **Technical Documentation**: This includes engineering drawings, specifications, and technical requirements that are crucial for identifying technical risks.

10. **Legal and Contractual Documents**: Contracts, agreements, and legal compliance documents are important for identifying legal and contractual risks.

11. **Environmental Studies**: For projects with environmental impacts, studies related to ecology, community impact, and sustainability are important.

12. **Market Analysis Reports**: These provide insights into market trends, competition, and economic factors that could pose external risks to the project.

By establishing these relevant documents at the beginning of the risk process, the risk management team can ensure a comprehensive approach to identifying, analyzing, and responding to project risks. This forms a solid foundation for effective risk management throughout the project lifecycle.

Performing a preliminary document analysis is an essential step in risk management, particularly in the context of project risk management as outlined in PMI standards. The following case study provides a practical application of this process.

CASE STUDY: CONSTRUCTION PROJECT RISK MANAGEMENT

Context

A construction company is embarking on a large-scale commercial building project. The project risk manager is tasked with conducting a preliminary document analysis to identify potential risks.

Preliminary Documents to Review

1. Industry Benchmarks:

- Sources: Industry reports, construction market analyses, and publications by construction associations.

- Content: Average project timelines, cost benchmarks, common risks in similar projects, and industry-wide safety standards.

2. Previous Lessons Learned:

- Sources: Company's past project reports, debriefing sessions, and internal risk management databases.

- Content: Challenges faced in similar past projects, effective risk mitigation strategies used, and areas where past projects overran in time or budget.

3. Historical Data:

- Sources: Internal project archives, financial records. and project performance data.

- Content: Data on project durations, cost variances, supplier performance, and previous risk occurrences.

4. External Sources:

- Sources: Government publications on construction standards, market trend reports, and economic forecasts.

- Content: Regulatory changes, economic trends affecting material costs, and labor market conditions.

Assigning Responsibility for Document Analysis

- **Project Manager:** Oversees the overall process, ensuring that the document analysis aligns with the project's objectives and scope.

- **Risk Manager:** Conducts a detailed review of the documents, focusing on identifying potential risks and their sources.

- **Financial Controller:** Analyzes financial and historical data to identify financial risks and their potential impact.

Establishing Relevant Documents

1. **Risk Identification Checklist:** A structured checklist based on the reviewed documents to systematically identify potential risks.

2. **Risk Register:** A document for recording identified risks, their sources, and potential impact on the project.

3. **Stakeholder Analysis:** A document identifying key stakeholders and their potential influence on risk factors.

Conclusion

In this case, the preliminary document analysis plays a crucial role in identifying potential risks before the project commences. By carefully reviewing industry benchmarks, lessons learned, historical data, and external sources, the project risk manager, in collaboration with the project manager and financial controller, establishes a solid foundation for effective risk management throughout the project lifecycle. This approach not only anticipates potential challenges but also equips the team with insights for proactive risk mitigation, aligning with the principles of the PMI standards for risk management.

Task 2 Assess project environment for threats and opportunities

SELECTION OF APPROPRIATE ORGANIZATIONAL PROCESS ASSETS, ENTERPRISE ENVIRONMENTAL FACTORS, AND PROJECT METHODOLOGIES

Determining the appropriate Organizational Process Assets (OPA), Enterprise Environmental Factors (EEF), and project methodology is a crucial aspect of assessing the project environment for threats and opportunities. This assessment is integral to Task 2 of Domain I in risk management planning.

1. **Organizational Process Assets (OPA)**: OPAs are the specific practices, procedures, policies, and knowledge bases specific to and used by the performing organization. These include but are not limited to:

- **Historical Information and Lessons Learned**: Past project documents and records that provide insights into risk management successes and failures.

- **Templates and Tools**: Existing risk management templates, tools, and software used in the organization.

- **Standards and Guidelines**: Organizational standards, policies, and guidelines relevant to project management and risk management.

The choice of OPAs should be aligned with the project's unique requirements and the organization's historical performance in similar projects.

2. **Enterprise Environmental Factors (EEF)**: EEFs are conditions, not under the immediate control of the team, that influence, constrain, or direct the project. These include:

- **Organizational Culture and Structure**: The organizational hierarchy, reporting structures, and cultural norms that can impact risk management approaches.

- **Market Conditions**: Current market trends, competition, and economic conditions that could influence project risks.

- **Regulatory Requirements**: Legal and regulatory constraints that the project must comply with.

- **Stakeholder Risk Tolerances**: The risk appetite of key stakeholders that can influence risk management strategies.

Understanding EEFs is vital in tailoring the risk management approach to the external environment in which the project operates.

3. **Project Methodology**: The choice of project methodology (agile, waterfall, hybrid, etc.) significantly impacts the risk management approach.

- **Agile Methodology**: Suitable for projects where requirements are expected to evolve. It allows for flexibility and iterative risk assessment.

- **Waterfall Methodology**: More appropriate for projects with well-defined requirements and scope. Risks are typically assessed and planned at the beginning of the project.

- **Hybrid Methodology**: Combines elements of both agile and waterfall methodologies. It can be tailored to fit the specific needs of the project, taking into account the strengths of both approaches.

The project methodology should be chosen based on the project's complexity, stakeholder requirements, deliverables, and the degree of uncertainty.

In summary, determining the right mix of OPAs, EEFs, and project methodology is essential for a robust risk assessment. It involves understanding the internal and external factors that influence the project, along with selecting a project management approach that aligns with these factors and the overall project objectives. This process sets the stage for identifying potential risks and opportunities and developing a comprehensive risk management plan.

ANALYSIS OF ENVIRONMENTAL FACTORS IN THE PLANNING PHASE

Analyzing environmental factors in the planning phase of a project is critical for identifying potential threats and opportunities. Tools like PESTLE and SWOT analyses offer structured methods to evaluate these factors systematically.

PESTLE Analysis

PESTLE analysis is a strategic tool used to understand the macro environmental factors that may impact a project. It stands for Political, Economic, Social, Technological, Legal, and Environmental factors.

1. **Political Factors**: Assess the impact of government policy, political stability or instability, tax guidelines, trade regulations, and other political dynamics.

2. **Economic Factors**: Consider economic conditions like inflation, interest rates, economic growth patterns, unemployment rates, and other market economics that can affect project funding, costs, and viability.

3. **Social Factors**: Analyze demographic changes, cultural trends, lifestyle shifts, education levels, and social attitudes that may influence the project's acceptance and success.

4. **Technological Factors**: Evaluate the impact of emerging or existing technologies, technological obsolescence, innovation, and IT infrastructure on the project.

5. **Legal Factors**: Examine legal requirements such as employment laws, health and safety regulations, consumer protection laws, and how they could impact the project.

6. **Environmental Factors**: Understand environmental aspects like sustainability, carbon footprint, waste disposal, and climate change, especially for projects with significant environmental interactions.

SWOT Analysis

SWOT analysis is a tool used to evaluate a project's internal strengths and weaknesses, and external opportunities and threats.

1. **Strengths**: Identify internal positive attributes of the project that can be leveraged to achieve project objectives. This could include a skilled team, strong financial resources, or advanced technology.

2. **Weaknesses**: Acknowledge internal factors that may hinder project success. These might include resource limitations, lack of expertise, or budget constraints.

3. **Opportunities**: Look for external factors that the project can capitalize on or use to its advantage, such as market gaps, regulatory changes, or technological advancements.

4. **Threats**: Recognize external factors that could jeopardize the project, like competitive pressures, changing market conditions, or supply chain disruptions.

Integration in Risk Management

Integrating PESTLE and SWOT analyses into the risk management planning phase helps in:

- **Comprehensive Risk Identification**: Ensures all relevant environmental factors are considered, leading to a more thorough risk identification process.

- **Strategic Decision Making**: Provides a strategic overview, guiding decision-makers in developing effective risk responses and strategies.

- **Adaptive Planning**: Helps in creating flexible plans that can adapt to changing environmental conditions.

In conclusion, a detailed analysis of environmental factors using PESTLE and SWOT tools is essential for an effective risk management process. It allows for a comprehensive understanding of the external and internal factors that can impact the project, thereby facilitating more informed and strategic risk management decisions.

ASSESSMENT OF ORGANIZATIONAL AND CULTURAL RISK APPETITE AND MATURITY

Determining the organizational and cultural risk appetite and analyzing the environment for risk culture maturity are key steps in the process of assessing a project's environment for threats and opportunities. These tasks involve understanding how much risk an organization is willing to accept and the degree to which its culture supports effective risk management practices.

Determining Organizational and Cultural Risk Appetite

1. **Definition of Risk Appetite**: Risk appetite refers to the amount and type of risk that an organization is prepared to pursue, retain, or accept. It is influenced by the organization's strategic objectives, market position, and stakeholder expectations.

2. Assessment Methods:

- **Review Strategic Documents**: Analyze the organization's mission, vision, and strategic objectives to infer the implied risk appetite.

- **Stakeholder Interviews**: Engage with key stakeholders, including senior management and board members, to understand their perspectives on risk-taking.

- **Historical Analysis**: Examine past decisions and project outcomes to gauge the organization's tolerance for risk.

3. Quantifying Risk Appetite:

- **Develop Risk Appetite Statements**: Create clear, quantifiable statements that define acceptable levels of risk in different areas (financial, operational, reputational).

- **Link to Objectives**: Ensure that the risk appetite aligns with the organization's overall objectives and capabilities.

Analyzing Environment for Risk Culture Maturity

1. **Definition of Risk Culture**: Risk culture refers to the values, beliefs, knowledge, and understanding about risk shared by a group of people with a common purpose, particularly the employees of an organization.

2. Assessment Aspects:

- **Risk Awareness**: Assess how well risks are understood across the organization. Do employees recognize risks in their day-to-day activities?

- **Communication**: Evaluate the effectiveness of risk-related communication. Is there a free flow of information about risks at all levels?

- **Training and Resources**: Determine if adequate training and resources are provided for effective risk management.

- **Leadership and Governance**: Observe the role of leadership in promoting risk management. Do leaders demonstrate a commitment to managing risk?

3. Tools for Assessment:

- **Surveys and Questionnaires**: Conduct surveys to gather employees' views on risk and their understanding of the organization's risk culture.

- **Focus Groups**: Hold focus group discussions to delve deeper into attitudes and perceptions about risk.

- **Risk Maturity Models**: Use maturity models to benchmark the organization's risk culture against best practices.

4. Actionable Insights:

- **Identify Gaps**: Highlight areas where the organization's risk culture needs improvement.

- **Develop Improvement Plans**: Create plans to address gaps, such as through enhanced training, communication strategies, or leadership engagement.

In summary, determining the organizational and cultural risk appetite involves understanding how much risk is acceptable in pursuit of strategic objectives, while analyzing risk culture maturity focuses on evaluating how well the organization's culture supports effective risk management. These assessments are critical for aligning risk management strategies with the organization's capacity and willingness to handle risks.

EVALUATION OF THE PROJECT MANAGEMENT INFORMATION SYSTEM (PMIS) PROCESSES AND DATA

Evaluating the project management information system (PMIS) process and data is an essential component in assessing a project's environment for risks. The PMIS is a system used for planning, executing, and closing project management goals. It typically includes tools and techniques used to gather, integrate, and disseminate the outputs of project management processes. Here's how you can approach the evaluation:

Key Aspects of PMIS Evaluation

1. System Functionality and Integration:

- **Tool Capabilities**: Assess the capabilities of the PMIS tools in use (like scheduling software, risk management tools, collaboration platforms). Are they adequately meeting the project needs?

- **Integration**: Examine how well these tools integrate with each other. Seamless integration is crucial for efficient information flow.

2. Data Quality and Accessibility:

- **Accuracy and Reliability**: Ensure that the data stored and processed in the PMIS is accurate, up-to-date, and reliable.

- **Accessibility**: Evaluate whether team members can access necessary information when needed. Also, consider the ease of use of the PMIS.

3. Security and Compliance:

- **Data Security**: Assess the security measures in place to protect sensitive project information.

- **Compliance**: Ensure that the PMIS is compliant with relevant legal and regulatory requirements, especially concerning data privacy.

4. Process Efficiency:

- **Workflow Efficiency**: Analyze how the PMIS supports or improves project workflows. Does it streamline tasks and facilitate better project management practices?

- **Bottlenecks and Limitations**: Identify any bottlenecks or limitations in the current processes that might hinder project progress.

5. Reporting and Analytics:

- **Reporting Features**: Evaluate the reporting capabilities of the PMIS. Can it generate useful, timely, and accurate reports?

- **Analytical Tools**: Assess whether the PMIS provides analytical tools for project performance tracking and forecasting.

6. User Experience and Training:

- **Ease of Use**: Consider the user-friendliness of the PMIS. A steep learning curve can hinder effective usage.

- **Training and Support**: Check if adequate training and support are provided to the users of the PMIS.

Alexander Stratton

7. Scalability and Flexibility:

- **Adaptability**: Determine if the PMIS can adapt to the changing needs of the project.

- **Scalability**: Assess whether the system can handle the project's growth in terms of size and complexity.

Risk Considerations

- **Technological Risks**: Be aware of risks associated with software failure, data corruption, or system incompatibilities.

- **Information Overload**: Too much data without adequate filtering or prioritization can lead to information overload, making it difficult to discern critical project insights.

- **User Adoption**: Resistance to new systems or processes can pose a significant risk to project success.

Conclusion

Evaluating the PMIS is not just about assessing the software tools but also about understanding how well they support the project management processes and the team's ability to deliver the project successfully. This evaluation helps in identifying potential risks associated with information management and technology, enabling the project team to take proactive measures to mitigate them.

EXECUTION OF COMPREHENSIVE STAKEHOLDER ANALYSIS

Conducting a stakeholder analysis is a fundamental aspect of risk management, particularly in identifying and understanding the various individuals or groups that have a stake in the project's outcome. This analysis helps in anticipating and managing the influences and concerns of stakeholders, which can significantly impact the project's success. Here's a structured approach to conducting a stakeholder analysis:

Steps in Stakeholder Analysis

1. Identify Stakeholders:

-   **List All Potential Stakeholders**: Include everyone who may affect or be affected by the project, such as team members, managers, customers, suppliers, regulators, and other external parties.

-   **Use Project Documentation**: Review project charters, contracts, and organizational documents to identify stakeholders.

2. Analyze Stakeholder Interests and Influence:

-   **Understand Their Interests**: Determine what each stakeholder expects from the project. What are their needs, interests, and concerns?

-   **Assess Their Influence**: Evaluate how much power and influence each stakeholder has over the project. Consider their authority level, resource control, and network.

3. Classify Stakeholders:

-   **Prioritize Stakeholders**: Use tools like Power/Interest grids to categorize stakeholders based on their level of interest and influence. This helps in prioritizing stakeholder engagement efforts.

-   **Group Similar Stakeholders**: Group stakeholders with similar interests and levels of influence. This can streamline communication and engagement strategies.

4. Understand Stakeholders' Risk Appetite:

-   **Assess Their Risk Tolerance**: Different stakeholders may have varying levels of risk tolerance. Understanding this helps tailor risk management strategies to address their concerns effectively.

5. Develop Engagement Strategies:

-   **Tailor Communication**: Develop communication plans that cater to the specific needs and expectations of each stakeholder group.

-   **Engage Actively**: Regularly engage with stakeholders through meetings, updates, and consultations to keep them informed and involved.

6. Monitor and Adjust:

-   **Review Stakeholder Positions**: Stakeholders' positions and interests may change over the project lifecycle. Regularly reassess and adjust your strategies accordingly.

- **Feedback Loops**: Establish mechanisms for stakeholders to provide feedback on the project's progress and risk management efforts.

Considerations in Risk Management

- **Stakeholder Conflicts**: Be aware of potential conflicts between stakeholders' interests and develop strategies to manage them.
- **Change in Stakeholder Dynamics**: Stay alert to changes in stakeholder dynamics, such as changes in organizational structure or stakeholder priorities.
- **Cultural Sensitivity**: In a global project environment, be mindful of cultural differences and how they might affect stakeholder interactions and expectations.

Conclusion

A thorough stakeholder analysis is vital for effective risk management. It enables the project team to understand and manage stakeholder expectations, align strategies with stakeholder needs, and proactively address potential risks arising from stakeholder interactions. This process is not a one-time activity but a continuous one, requiring regular updates and adjustments throughout the project lifecycle.

ANALYSIS OF CONSTRAINTS IMPACTING RISK MANAGEMENT

Analyzing constraints to risk management is a vital task in project management, particularly in recognizing and understanding the limitations and challenges that can impede effective risk management practices. These constraints can arise from various sources such as government regulations, market conditions, organizational structures, environmental factors, and technical limitations. Here's a comprehensive approach to analyzing these constraints:

Government Constraints

1. Regulatory Compliance:

- **Legal Regulations**: Understand the legal frameworks and regulations that the project must adhere to. Non-compliance can result in legal risks, fines, or project shutdowns.

- **Permitting and Licensing**: Identify the necessary permits and licenses required for the project. Delays in obtaining these can pose risks to project timelines.

2. Political Environment

- **Political Stability**: Evaluate the impact of political stability or instability in the project's region.

- **Policy Changes**: Be aware of potential changes in government policies that could affect the project.

Market Laws/Rules Constraints

1. Industry Standards:

- **Compliance with Standards**: Identify industry-specific standards and ensure the project aligns with these requirements.

- **Market Trends**: Keep abreast of market trends that can influence project success, such as shifts in consumer behavior or technological advancements.

2. Economic Conditions:

- **Market Volatility**: Consider risks associated with economic downturns or market volatility.

- **Supply Chain Dependencies**: Analyze the stability and reliability of supply chains, as disruptions can pose significant risks.

Organizational Constraints

1. Resource Limitations:

- **Budgetary Constraints**: Assess the impact of budget limitations on project scope and quality.

- **Personnel Resources**: Evaluate the availability and skills of personnel required for the project.

2. Organizational Culture:

- **Risk Tolerance**: Understand the organization's risk tolerance and how it impacts risk management decisions.

- **Internal Processes**: Examine internal processes and procedures that may hinder efficient risk management.

Environmental Constraints

1. Physical and Ecological Impact:

- **Environmental Regulations**: Comply with environmental laws and regulations to avoid legal and reputational risks.

- **Sustainability Practices**: Integrate sustainable practices to mitigate environmental risks.

2. Geographical Factors:

- **Location-specific Risks**: Consider risks associated with the project's geographical location, such as natural disasters.

Technical Constraints

1. Technology Limitations:

- **Technological Reliability**: Assess the reliability and suitability of the technology used in the project.

- **Innovation and Obsolescence**: Be aware of the risks associated with rapid technological change and obsolescence.

2. Data and Information Systems:

- **Data Security**: Evaluate the risks associated with data breaches and cybersecurity threats.

- **System Integrations**: Consider the challenges and risks associated with integrating new systems into existing infrastructures.

Conclusion

Analyzing these constraints is crucial in developing a comprehensive risk management plan. It involves a detailed examination of external and internal factors that can limit or challenge the effectiveness of risk management efforts. Understanding these constraints allows for more realistic planning, the development of contingency strategies, and proactive management of potential risks. This analysis should be an ongoing process, revisited throughout the project lifecycle to adapt to changing circumstances.

CULTIVATING A RISK AWARENESS CULTURE AMONG STAKEHOLDERS

Focusing stakeholders on creating a culture of risk awareness is a crucial task in risk management. This involves engaging and educating stakeholders about the importance of risk management, and fostering an environment where risks are openly discussed, understood, and managed effectively. Here are key strategies to cultivate a risk-aware culture among stakeholders:

1. Communication and Engagement:

- **Regular Communication**: Establish regular and transparent communication channels to discuss risk-related issues.

- **Inclusive Discussions**: Involve stakeholders in risk identification, analysis, and response planning processes.

2. Education and Training:

- **Tailored Training Sessions**: Conduct training sessions to educate stakeholders on risk management concepts, tools, and their roles in the process.

- **Customized Workshops**: Organize workshops that are tailored to the specific needs and levels of understanding of different stakeholder groups.

3. Demonstrating Leadership Commitment:

- **Leadership Involvement**: Ensure that project leaders and senior management actively participate in and endorse risk management activities.

- **Leading by Example**: Leaders should model risk-aware behaviors and decision-making processes.

4. Incorporating Risk Awareness into Organizational Culture:

- **Policy Integration**: Integrate risk management principles into organizational policies and procedures.

- **Reward and Recognition Systems**: Implement systems that recognize and reward risk-aware behaviors and effective risk management practices.

5. Stakeholder Empowerment:

- **Decision-Making Involvement**: Empower stakeholders to be part of the risk management decision-making process.

- **Encouraging Openness**: Foster an environment where stakeholders feel comfortable raising concerns and suggesting improvements.

6. Utilizing Real-world Examples:

- **Case Studies**: Use case studies and examples from within and outside the organization to illustrate the impact of effective risk management.

- **Lessons Learned**: Share lessons learned from past projects to highlight the importance of risk awareness.

7. Continuous Improvement:

- **Feedback Mechanisms**: Implement mechanisms for stakeholders to provide feedback on risk management practices.

- **Regular Reviews**: Conduct regular reviews and assessments of risk management activities and stakeholder engagement effectiveness.

8. Aligning Risk Management with Organizational Goals:

- **Strategic Alignment**: Clearly communicate how risk management contributes to achieving the organization's strategic objectives.

- **Relating to Individual Roles**: Help stakeholders understand how risk management relates to their specific roles and responsibilities.

Conclusion

Creating a culture of risk awareness among stakeholders is not a one-time event but an ongoing process. It requires consistent effort, strong leadership, and a strategic approach to embedding risk management into the fabric of the organization. By fostering open communication, providing education and training, empowering stakeholders, and demonstrating leadership commitment, an organization can build a strong, risk-aware culture that enhances its capacity to manage risks effectively.

IDENTIFICATION OF BUSINESS DRIVERS AND KEY ASSUMPTIONS IN PROJECT REALIZATION

Determining the business driver of a project, along with its key assumptions, benefits, and materialization, is an essential aspect of risk management. This process involves identifying the primary reasons behind initiating the project, outlining the expected benefits, and understanding the underlying assumptions that support the project's feasibility and success. Here's a structured approach to this task:

1. Identifying the Business Driver

- **Strategic Alignment**: Understand how the project aligns with the broader strategic goals of the organization. What strategic objectives does the project support or fulfill?

- **Market Demand**: Evaluate if the project is driven by market needs, customer demands, or a competitive strategy.

- **Regulatory Requirement**: Determine if the project is a response to new regulations or compliance requirements.

- **Operational Efficiency**: Assess if the project aims to improve operational efficiency, reduce costs, or enhance productivity.

- **Technological Advancement**: Consider if the project is driven by the need to adopt new technologies or innovation.

2. Outlining Key Assumptions

- **Market Assumptions**: Assumptions about market trends, customer behavior, and demand.

- **Resource Assumptions**: Availability and capability of resources required for the project.

- **Timeline Assumptions**: Estimated timeframes for project milestones and completion.

- **Cost Assumptions**: Assumptions regarding the project's budget and financial projections.

- **Technology Assumptions**: Assumptions about the technology to be used, its capabilities, and integration.

3. Defining Expected Benefits

- **Financial Benefits**: Increased revenue, cost savings, return on investment (ROI).

- **Customer Satisfaction**: Improved service quality, customer experience, or product value.

- **Operational Benefits**: Enhanced efficiency, productivity, or process improvements.

- **Strategic Benefits**: Advancement of organizational goals, market positioning, or competitive advantage.

- **Compliance and Risk Mitigation**: Meeting regulatory requirements and reducing operational risks.

4. Understanding Materialization of the Project

- **Realization Plan**: Develop a plan for how and when the project's benefits will be realized. This includes post-project evaluations to measure success.

- **Monitoring Mechanisms**: Implement mechanisms to monitor the project's progress towards achieving its stated benefits.

- **Contingency Plans**: Prepare for scenarios where key assumptions may prove incorrect or benefits may not materialize as expected.

Conclusion

Determining the business driver, assumptions, benefits, and materialization plan of a project provides a clear understanding of why the project is being undertaken and what it aims to achieve. This clarity is crucial for effective risk management, as it guides the identification and prioritization of risks and informs decision-making throughout the project lifecycle. It also ensures that all stakeholders have a shared understanding of the project's objectives and expected outcomes.

CASE STUDY: SOFTWARE DEVELOPMENT PROJECT IN A MULTINATIONAL CORPORATION

Context

A multinational corporation is initiating a software development project aimed at enhancing its customer relationship management system. The project risk manager is tasked with assessing the project environment for threats and opportunities.

Determining OPA / EEF / Project Methodology

- **Organizational Process Assets (OPA):** Company's existing project management templates, historical information, and lessons learned.

- **Enterprise Environmental Factors (EEF):** Organizational culture, market conditions, and technological advancements.

- **Project Methodology:** Given the nature of software development, a hybrid methodology combining Agile (for flexibility and adaptability) and Waterfall (for structured phases, especially in the integration with existing systems) is chosen.

Environmental Factors Analysis

- **PESTLE Analysis:** Political stability affecting market operations, economic trends influencing budgeting, social factors impacting user acceptance, technological advancements, legal compliance requirements, and environmental sustainability practices.

- **SWOT Analysis:** Strengths (experienced team, strong financial backing), weaknesses (possible resistance to change), opportunities (market leadership through technology), and threats (rapid technological obsolescence).

Organizational and Cultural Risk Appetite

- **Risk Culture Maturity:** Assessing the organization's history of risk taking, decision-making processes, and previous project outcomes.

- **Risk Appetite:** The corporation is moderately risk-averse, favoring calculated risks with clear ROI.

Alexander Stratton

Evaluating Project Management Information System (PMIS)

- **Process and Data Analysis:** Reviewing the effectiveness of existing PMIS tools in tracking project progress, resource allocation, and risk monitoring.

Conducting Stakeholder Analysis

- Identification of key stakeholders: project team, end-users, IT department, senior management.

- Assessing stakeholder's influence, interest, and potential impact on the project.

Analyzing Constraints to Risk Management

- **Government and Market Laws/Rules:** Compliance with data protection laws and software licensing.

- **Organizational Constraints:** Internal policies and resource limitations.

- **Environmental and Technical Risks:** Dependence on stable internet connectivity and compatibility with existing systems.

Cultivating Risk Awareness Among Stakeholders

- Implementing regular risk awareness workshops and including risk management in stakeholder communications.

Determining Business Driver of Project

- **Key Assumptions:** User requirements will remain stable; technology chosen will be scalable.

- **Benefits:** Improved customer satisfaction increased operational efficiency.

- **Materialization of Project:** Expected to integrate seamlessly with existing systems and yield a measurable increase in customer engagement.

Conclusion

In this case, a comprehensive assessment of the project environment for threats and opportunities is crucial for the successful implementation of the software development project. This involves a meticulous examination of organizational and environmental factors, stakeholder analysis, and an understanding of the business drivers. By focusing on creating a culture of risk awareness and analyzing constraints, the project team can navigate potential risks effectively. Aligning with PMI standards, this approach ensures that the project is well-positioned to adapt tc changes and capitalize on opportunities, thereby enhancing the overall success and sustainability of the project.

Task 3 Confirm risk thresholds based on risk appetites

ALIGNMENT OF PROJECT RISK THRESHOLDS WITH ORGANIZATIONAL RISK APPETITE

Aligning project risk thresholds to the organizational risk appetite is a critical step in Task 3 of risk management. This alignment ensures that the project's risk-taking levels are consistent with the broader risk tolerance of the organization. Here's how to approach this alignment:

Understanding Organizational Risk Appetite

- **Definition and Documentation**: Start by understanding the organization's risk appetite, which is typically documented in risk management policies or strategic planning documents. This appetite defines the level and type of risk the organization is willing to accept in pursuit of its objectives.

- **Engagement with Leadership**: Engage with senior management and key stakeholders to gain insights into the organization's strategic goals and how risk tolerance aligns with these goals.

Establishing Project Risk Thresholds

- **Risk Threshold Definition**: Risk thresholds are specific points at which the risk level becomes unacceptable. For a project, these thresholds are set based on various factors such as cost, time, scope, quality, and compliance.

- **Quantitative and Qualitative Measures**: Use both quantitative measures (like financial limits) and qualitative assessments (like reputational impact) to establish these thresholds.

Aligning with Organizational Appetite

1. **Consistency with Organizational Goals**: Ensure that the project's risk thresholds do not exceed the organization's overall risk appetite. The project's risk-taking should be in line with what the organization as a whole can bear and is willing to accept.

2. Alignment Across Various Risks:

- **Financial Risks**: Align the project's financial risk thresholds with the organization's financial stability and risk-bearing capacity.

- **Operational Risks**: Ensure that operational risk thresholds do not jeopardize the organization's operational integrity and efficiency.

- **Strategic Risks**: The project's strategic risk thresholds should support the organization's long-term strategic objectives.

3. **Sector-Specific and Regulatory Considerations**: In industries with specific regulatory requirements or high-risk sectors, ensure that risk thresholds are set in compliance with these external factors and industry norms.

4. **Feedback and Adjustments**: Continuously gather feedback from project stakeholders and the broader organization to ensure that risk thresholds remain aligned over time, especially in response to changing internal and external environments.

Conclusion

Aligning project risk thresholds with the organizational risk appetite is an exercise in balancing the project's objectives with the organization's capacity and willingness to take on risk. It requires a deep understanding of both the project-specific risks and the broader risk context of the organization. This alignment is critical for ensuring that the project advances organizational goals without exposing it to undue risk. Regular reviews and adjustments to these thresholds may be necessary as the project progresses and as external and internal factors evolve.

CALCULATION OF ORGANIZATIONAL RISK ABSORPTION CAPACITY

Calculating the risk that an organization can absorb involves a comprehensive assessment across various domains such as financial, scope, environmental, technical, legal, schedule, quality, and contractual aspects. This process is essential in understanding the organization's capacity to withstand and manage risks without significantly impacting its strategic objectives. Here's how to approach this calculation:

1. Financial Risk Absorption:

- **Assess Financial Health**: Review the organization's financial statements to understand its capital reserves, cash flow, and profitability.

- **Determine Financial Thresholds**: Set financial limits for risk exposure, considering the organization's capacity to absorb financial losses without jeopardizing its financial stability.

2. Scope Risk Absorption:

- **Scope Flexibility**: Evaluate the flexibility of the project scope. Can the project withstand changes without impacting the overall objectives?

- **Impact Analysis**: Conduct impact analysis to understand how scope changes could affect project deliverables and outcomes.

3. Environmental Risk Absorption:

- **Regulatory Compliance**: Ensure that environmental risks are within regulatory limits.

- **Sustainability Assessment**: Evaluate the organization's capacity to manage environmental risks while maintaining sustainable practices.

4. Technical Risk Absorption:

- **Technology Assessment**: Assess the reliability and maturity of the technology being used. Consider the organization's capacity to manage technical failures or setbacks.

- **Innovation and Adaptability**: Evaluate the organization's ability to adapt to technological changes or innovations.

5. Legal Risk Absorption:

- **Legal Compliance**: Determine the organization's ability to comply with legal and regulatory requirements.

- **Litigation Reserves**: Consider the organization's capacity to handle legal disputes, including the availability of legal reserves or insurance.

6. Schedule Risk Absorption:

- **Timeline Flexibility**: Assess the impact of schedule delays on the project and the organization.

- **Buffer Planning**: Calculate the buffer time available in project scheduling that can absorb delays without impacting critical milestones.

7. Quality Risk Absorption:

- **Quality Standards**: Understand the minimum quality standards required for project deliverables.

- **Quality Impact Assessment**: Analyze the implications of quality risks on the project and the organization's reputation.

8. Contractual Risk Absorption:

- **Contractual Obligations**: Review existing contracts for obligations and liabilities.

- **Contractual Flexibility**: Assess the organization's ability to negotiate or re-negotiate contracts in response to changes.

9. Consolidating Risk Absorption Capacity:

- **Aggregate Assessment**: Combine assessments from all areas to determine the overall risk absorption capacity of the organization.

- **Scenario Analysis**: Use scenario planning to evaluate how different risk events might impact the organization across these domains.

Conclusion

Calculating the risk absorption capacity of an organization requires a multi-faceted approach, considering financial, operational, and strategic aspects. It's important to not only look at each area in isolation but also understand the interdependencies and cumulative impact of risks across these areas. This comprehensive assessment helps in setting realistic risk thresholds and developing effective risk management strategies.

EXPLORATION AND DISCUSSION OF RISK THRESHOLDS

Discussing risk thresholds involves understanding and defining the specific points at which risk levels become unacceptable or require specific actions. Risk thresholds are essential in risk management as they provide clear criteria for when to implement risk responses. This concept is integral to the decision-making process in project management, guiding teams on when to act to mitigate or avoid risks. Here's a detailed discussion on risk thresholds:

Definition and Purpose

- **Risk Thresholds Defined**: Risk thresholds are pre-defined levels of risk exposure at which actions must be taken. They are quantifiable and can be set for different aspects of a project, such as cost, time, scope, quality, and compliance.

- **Purpose**: The primary purpose of setting risk thresholds is to establish clear boundaries for acceptable risk levels, enabling proactive risk management and ensuring that risks are managed within tolerable limits.

Setting Risk Thresholds

1. **Alignment with Risk Appetite**: Risk thresholds should align with the organization's overall risk appetite, reflecting how much risk is acceptable in pursuit of project objectives.

2. **Quantitative and Qualitative Criteria**: They can be based on quantitative measures (like a specific cost overrun percentage) or qualitative criteria (such as reputational impact).

3. **Consideration of Project Variables**: Different projects may have varying thresholds based on their specific characteristics, such as complexity, duration, and sensitivity.

Importance in Risk Management

1. **Early Warning System**: Risk thresholds serve as an early warning system, signaling when risks are approaching unacceptable levels.

2. **Decision-Making Framework**: They provide a framework for making informed decisions about whether to accept, mitigate, transfer, or avoid risks.

3. **Resource Allocation**: Helps in prioritizing resources for risk management activities based on the severity and proximity of risks to these thresholds.

Communicating Risk Thresholds

- **Stakeholder Involvement**: Engage stakeholders in setting and reviewing risk thresholds to ensure their understanding and buy-in.

- **Transparency**: Maintain transparency in how thresholds are determined and communicated to all relevant parties involved in the project.

Monitoring and Adjusting

1. **Regular Monitoring**: Risk thresholds should be monitored regularly to ensure they remain relevant and effective.

2. **Dynamic Adjustment**: They may need to be adjusted in response to changes in the project's environment, scope, or objectives.

Challenges

- **Setting Realistic Thresholds**: Determining thresholds that are neither too conservative nor too liberal can be challenging.

- **Subjectivity**: In cases of qualitative thresholds, subjectivity can lead to inconsistent interpretations.

- **Comprehensive Coverage**: Ensuring all critical aspects of the project have appropriately set thresholds.

Conclusion

Risk thresholds are a key component of effective risk management. They provide actionable criteria for responding to risks and help maintain project objectives within acceptable risk levels. Properly set and managed thresholds contribute significantly to the project's overall success by enabling timely and informed decision-making.

FACILITATION OF STAKEHOLDER CONFLICT RESOLUTION IN RISK APPETITE AGREEMENT

Leading conflict resolution among stakeholders in agreeing on risk appetite is a vital aspect of risk management, especially given that different stakeholders often have varying perspectives and tolerances for risk. This process involves navigating disagreements and finding a consensus or a mutually acceptable approach to risk-taking. Here's how to effectively lead this process:

Understanding Stakeholder Perspectives

1. **Identify Stakeholder Positions**: Begin by identifying the risk appetite of each stakeholder. Understand their concerns, motivations, and how the project's risks impact them.

2. **Acknowledge Differences**: Recognize that differences in risk appetite can stem from various factors like departmental objectives, personal experiences, and professional backgrounds.

Effective Communication

1. **Open Dialogue**: Foster an environment where stakeholders feel comfortable expressing their views on risk. Encourage open and honest discussions.

2. **Clarify Misunderstandings**: Often, conflicts arise from misunderstandings. Ensure that all stakeholders have a clear understanding of the risks, their implications, and how they are being measured and managed.

Facilitating Discussions

1. **Structured Meetings**: Organize structured discussions focused on risk appetite. Use these meetings to explore different perspectives and the rationale behind them.

2. **Neutral Facilitation**: Act as a neutral facilitator or consider bringing in an external mediator to ensure that discussions are balanced and productive.

Developing a Consensus

1. **Explore Common Ground**: Identify areas of agreement among stakeholders. Often, there are shared objectives or concerns that can serve as a starting point for building consensus.

2. **Compromise and Negotiation**: Encourage stakeholders to negotiate and compromise. This might involve balancing more conservative and aggressive risk stances.

Educational Approach

1. **Risk Management Education**: Sometimes, stakeholders might not have a deep understanding of risk management principles. Provide educational resources or sessions to enhance their understanding.

2. **Scenario Analysis**: Use scenario planning and analysis to demonstrate the potential impact of different risk levels. This can help stakeholders visualize and understand the implications of various risk appetites.

Decision-Making Framework

1. **Criteria for Decision-Making**: Establish criteria that will guide the decision-making process. This might include the strategic goals of the organization, project objectives, and regulatory requirements.

2. **Voting or Consensus Building**: Depending on the organizational culture, use a democratic voting system or a consensus-building approach to finalize the decision on risk appetite.

Documenting Agreements

1. **Formal Documentation**: Once a consensus is reached, document the agreed-upon risk appetite. This ensures clarity and serves as a reference point for future decisions.

2. **Review Mechanisms**: Set up regular reviews of the risk appetite agreement, as risk tolerances and project environments can change over time.

Conclusion

Resolving conflicts over risk appetite among stakeholders is a delicate process that requires diplomacy, effective communication, and a deep understanding of the different perspectives involved. It's about finding a balance between various risk tolerances while aligning with the overall project and organizational objectives. Maintaining flexibility and openness to adjustments as the project evolves is also crucial.

CASE STUDY: INFRASTRUCTURE DEVELOPMENT IN AN ENERGY COMPANY

Context

An energy company is embarking on a large-scale infrastructure development project, involving the construction of new facilities and upgrading existing ones. The project risk manager is responsible for confirming risk thresholds based on the organization's risk appetite.

Aligning Project Risk Thresholds to Organizational Risk Appetite

- **Assessment of Organizational Risk Appetite:** The company has a moderate risk appetite, prioritizing safety and regulatory compliance while being open to calculated risks for innovation and efficiency.

- **Alignment with Project:** The risk thresholds for the project are set to align with this moderate risk appetite, focusing on high safety standards, regulatory compliance, and efficient resource management.

Calculating the Risk the Organization Can Absorb

- **Financial Risk:** Evaluating the maximum budget variance the organization can tolerate without affecting its financial stability.

- **Scope Risk:** Assessing the flexibility in project scope without impacting core objectives.

- **Environmental Risk:** Ensuring compliance with environmental regulations and the company's commitment to sustainability.

- **Technical Risk:** Determining the extent of technical challenges the project can handle, considering the team's expertise and available technology.

- **Legal Risk:** Identifying legal constraints, including contract obligations and regulatory compliance.

- **Schedule Risk:** Estimating the maximum delay in project timelines that can be accommodated without significant impact.

- **Quality Risk:** Setting standards for acceptable quality levels that align with the company's reputation and customer expectations.

- **Contract Risk:** Understanding the implications of contractual agreements and their impact on the project.

Discussing Risk Thresholds

- **Stakeholder Meetings:** Organizing meetings with key stakeholders to present and discuss the calculated risk thresholds.

- **Documentation:** Providing a detailed analysis of how these thresholds were determined and their implications on the project.

Leading Conflict Resolutions

- **Facilitating Dialogues:** Encouraging open discussions among stakeholders with differing views on the risk appetite.

- **Mediation Techniques:** Using mediation techniques to address conflicts and find a middle ground that aligns with the organizational risk appetite.

- **Decision-Making Frameworks:** Implementing structured decision-making frameworks to guide the resolution process.

Conclusion

In this case, confirming risk thresholds based on the energy company's risk appetites involves a detailed analysis of various risk aspects, including financial, scope, environmental, technical, legal, schedule, and quality risks. Aligning project risk thresholds with the organizational risk appetite is crucial for ensuring that the infrastructure development project proceeds in a manner that is both ambitious and within the bounds of acceptable risk. Facilitating stakeholder discussions and leading conflict resolutions are key components in agreeing on a shared understanding of risk appetite. This structured approach aligns with PMI standards and ensures that the project is managed in a way that respects both the company's risk tolerance and its strategic objectives.

Task 4 Establish risk management strategy

IMPLEMENTATION OF RISK MANAGEMENT PROCESSES AND TOOLS

Establishing risk processes and tools is a fundamental part of Task 4 in risk management strategy. This step involves setting up structured methods and implementing tools that facilitate effective risk identification, analysis, response, and monitoring. Here's a guide to establishing these processes and tools:

Establishing Risk Processes

1. Risk Identification Process:

- **Define Methods**: Choose methods for identifying risks, such as brainstorming sessions, expert interviews, and analysis of historical data.

- **Involvement Protocols**: Establish who should be involved in the risk identification process, including stakeholders, project team members, and external experts.

2. Risk Analysis Process:

- **Qualitative and Quantitative Techniques**: Implement both qualitat ve (like risk probability and impact assessment) and quantitative (such as Monte Carlo simulations) analysis techniques.

- **Criteria for Evaluation**: Develop criteria for evaluating and prioritizing risks, considering factors like likelihood, impact, and urgency.

3. Risk Response Planning:

- **Response Strategies**: Outline standard response strategies for different types of risks (avoid, mitgate, transfer, accept).

- **Action Plans**: Develop action plans for high-priority risks, detailing the steps to be taken, responsible individuals, and timelines.

4. Risk Monitoring and Review:

- **Tracking Mechanisms**: Set up processes for tracking identified risks and monitoring the effectiveness of risk responses.

- **Review Schedules**: Establish regular intervals for reviewing and updating the risk management plan.

Implementing Risk Management Tools

1. **Risk Register**: Implement a risk register tool that records all identified risks, their analysis, and response plans. This can be a simple spreadsheet or a specialized software tool.

2. **Project Management Software**: Utilize project management software that includes risk management features, allowing for integration with other project activities.

3. **Analytical Tools**: Employ tools for risk analysis, such as statistical software for quantitative risk analysis or decision-making software for qualitative assessments.

4. **Reporting Tools**: Use reporting tools that enable the creation of risk reports and dashboards for easy visualization and communication of risk status.

5. **Collaboration Platforms**: Implement collaboration platforms that allow team members to communicate and share information on risk management activities easily.

Best Practices

- **Customization**: Tailor the risk management processes and tools to fit the specific needs and complexity of the project.

- **Integration**: Ensure that risk management processes are integrated with other project management processes.

- **Training**: Provide training for the project team on how to use the risk management tools and follow the established processes.

- **Continuous Improvement**: Regularly review and update the processes and tools based on lessons learned and feedback from the team.

Conclusion

Establishing effective risk processes and tools is key to a robust risk management strategy. It ensures that risks are systematically identified, analyzed, responded to, and monitored throughout the project lifecycle. The choice and implementation of these processes and tools should consider the specific context of the project and the organization, aiming for an integrated and dynamic approach to managing risks.

PROVISION OF RISK MANAGEMENT TEMPLATES AND FORMS

Providing risk management templates and forms is an important aspect of establishing a risk management strategy. These templates and forms standardize the process of risk identification, assessment, and response, ensuring consistency and efficiency across the project. Here's a guide to some essential risk management templates and forms that can be provided:

1. Risk Register Template

- **Purpose**: To document and track all identified risks, their analysis, response strategies, and monitoring status.

- Key Elements:

- Risk ID and Description

- Risk Category (e.g., financial, operational, technical)

- Probability and Impact Assessment

- Risk Owner

- Proposed Response Strategies (avoid, mitigate, transfer, accept)

- Status of Risk (open, closed, in progress)

- Monitoring and Review Notes

2. Risk Assessment Matrix

- **Purpose**: To assist in evaluating the severity of risks based on their likelihood and impact.
- Key Elements:
- Likelihood Scale (e.g.. Low, Medium, High)
- Impact Scale (e.g., Low, Medium, High)
- Risk Rating (combination of likelihood and impact)

3. Risk Response Plan Template

- **Purpose**: To detail the action plan for each high-priority risk.
- Key Elements:
- Risk ID and Description
- Selected Response Strategy
- Specific Actions to Implement the Strategy
- Responsible Individuals or Teams
- Timeline for Response Implementation
- Contingency Plans

4. Risk Review Form

- **Purpose**: To facilitate the regular review and update of the risk management plan.
- Key Elements:
- Date of Review
- Reviewer's Name and Role
- Changes in Risk Status
- Effectiveness of Risk Responses
- Adjustments Needed
- Next Review Date

5. Stakeholder Risk Analysis Form

- **Purpose**: To analyze and document risks related to stakeholders.
- Key Elements:

- Stakeholder Identification
- Potential Risk Associated with Each Stakeholder
- Impact on Stakeholder
- Stakeholder's Influence on Project
- Strategies for Stakeholder Engagement

6. Risk Reporting Template

- **Purpose**: To create standardized reports for communicating risk status to stakeholders.
- Key Elements:
- Reporting Period
- Summary of Key Risks
- Changes in Risk Profile
- Summary of Risk Responses Implemented
- Recommendations for Further Action

Best Practices

- **Customizability**: Ensure that templates are customizable to fit the specific needs of different projects.
- **User-Friendly Design**: Design templates to be intuitive and easy to use, even for those with limited risk management experience.
- **Integration with Other Tools**: Templates should be compatible with other project management software and tools used by the organization.

Conclusion

Providing well-structured risk management templates and forms is essential for effective risk management. These tools facilitate a systematic approach to identifying, assessing, and managing risks and ensure that all team members are on the same page regarding risk management practices. Regular training and updates on these templates can further enhance their effectiveness and utility in managing project risks.

DETERMINATION OF RISK METRICS

Determining risk metrics is an essential step in the risk management process providing a means to quantify and monitor risks systematically. These metrics are used to assess the likelihood and impact of risks, measure the effectiveness of risk responses, and track risk trends over time. Here's a guide to determining effective risk metrics:

1. Risk Probability and Impact

- **Probability Rating**: A metric to quantify the likelihood of a risk occurring, typically expressed as a percentage or on a scale (e.g., low, medium, high).

- **Impact Rating**: A measure of the potential effect of a risk on project objectives, which could be in terms of cost, time, scope, quality, or reputation.

2. Risk Exposure or Risk Score

- **Calculation**: Multiply the probability rating by the impact rating to get a risk score. This quantifies the overall exposure of the risk.

- **Usage**: Helps prioritize risks based on their severity.

3. Risk Velocity

- **Definition**: The speed at which a risk can impact a project.

- **Application**: Useful in understanding the urgency of risk response measures.

4. Risk Appetite Metrics

- **Tolerance Levels**: Establish quantitative thresholds for acceptable levels of risk in various areas (financial, operational, compliance, etc.).

- **Alignment**: Ensure these metrics align with the organization's overall risk appetite.

5. Value at Risk (VaR)

- **Description**: A statistical technique used to measure the maximum potential loss over a specified time period at a given confidence level.

- **Context**: Commonly used in financial risk management.

6. Risk Mitigation Effectiveness

- **Measurement**: Assess the effectiveness of risk responses in reducing the probability and/or impact of risks.

- **Indicators**: Include changes in risk scores post-mitigation.

7. Residual Risk Level

- **After Mitigation**: The level of risk remaining after risk responses have been implemented.

- **Tracking**: Monitor residual risks to ensure they stay within acceptable limits.

8. Key Risk Indicators (KRIs)

- **Early Warning Signals**: Develop indicators that provide early warnings of increasing risk exposure.

- **Examples**: Could include metrics like cost variance, schedule variance, employee turnover rates, or supplier delivery times.

9. Risk Concentration

- **Analysis**: Identify areas where risks are concentrated (e.g., in certain project phases, processes, or geographical locations).

- **Purpose**: To ensure that risk mitigation efforts are properly diversified.

Best Practices

- **Relevance and Simplicity**: Choose metrics that are relevant to the project's context and keep them simple for ease of understanding and tracking.

- **Regular Reviews**: Risk metrics should be reviewed regularly to ensure they remain applicable and are effectively tracking risk exposure.

- **Stakeholder Involvement**: Engage stakeholders in determining and reviewing risk metrics to ensure alignment with their expectations and concerns.

Conclusion

Risk metrics are vital for quantifying, monitoring, and managing risks in a structured manner. They provide a common language for discussing risks and facilitate informed decision-making. The choice of risk metrics should be tailored to the specific needs of the project and the organization, and they should be regularly reviewed and updated as the project evolves.

IDENTIFICATION OF RISK CATEGORIES

Identifying risk categories is an integral part of establishing a risk management strategy. Risk categories help in organizing and grouping risks, making it easier to identify, analyze, and manage them effectively. By categorizing risks, you can apply specialized risk management approaches relevant to each category and better allocate resources. Here's a guide to identifying common risk categories in project management:

1. Strategic Risks

- **Description**: Risks that affect the organization's ability to achieve its strategic objectives.

- **Examples**: Changes in market conditions, competitive pressures, or strategic decision errors.

2. Operational Risks

- **Description**: Risks arising from the day-to-day operational activities of the organization.

- **Examples**: Process inefficiencies, system failures, or human errors.

3. Financial Risks

- **Description**: Risks related to the financial aspects of the project or organization.

- **Examples**: Budget overruns, cash flow issues, or changes in interest rates.

4. Market Risks

- **Description**: Risks associated with the market environment in which the organization operates.

- **Examples**: Fluctuations in demand, price changes, or economic downturns.

5. Compliance and Legal Risks

- **Description**: Risks related to legal and regulatory requirements.

- **Examples**: Non-compliance penalties, legal disputes, or changes in regulations.

6. Technology Risks

- **Description**: Risks associated with the use of technology in a project.

Alexander Stratton

- **Examples**: Cybersecurity threats, technological obsolescence, or system malfunctions.

7. Environmental Risks

- **Description**: Risks related to the physical environment.

- **Examples**: Natural disasters, climate change impacts, or environmental accidents.

8. Project Management Risks

- **Description**: Risks specifically related to the management of the project.

- **Examples**: Scope creep, inadequate resource allocation, or communication breakdowns.

9. Human Resource Risks

- **Description**: Risks arising from the workforce involved in the project.

- **Examples**: Staff turnover, lack of training, or labor disputes.

10. Reputational Risks

- **Description**: Risks that could adversely affect the perception of stakeholders.

- **Examples**: Public relations issues, customer dissatisfaction, or negative social media exposure.

11. Supply Chain Risks

- **Description**: Risks related to the supply chain and logistics.

- **Examples**: Supplier failure, transportation delays, or inventory problems.

Best Practices

- **Tailor Categories to the Project**: Customize the risk categories to the specific nature and context of the project.

- **Overlapping Risks**: Be aware of risks that may fall into multiple categories and ensure they are managed appropriately.

- **Dynamic Categorization**: Update and revise risk categories as the project evolves and new information emerges.

Conclusion

Identifying and categorizing risks is a foundational step in risk management that facilitates a structured and efficient approach to risk assessment and mitigation. It aids in understanding the diverse nature of risks and in applying targeted risk management strategies for each category. Regular reviews and updates to these categories are important as the project progresses and new risks emerge.

FACILITATION OF RISK MANAGEMENT COACHING AND MENTORING USING SERVANT LEADERSHIP PRINCIPLES

Coaching and mentoring a team on risk management best practices, especially within the framework of servant leadership, involves guiding the team not only in the technical aspects of risk management but also in fostering a culture of teamwork, responsibility, and proactive risk handling. Here's how to approach this task:

Understanding Servant Leadership in Risk Management

- **Servant Leadership Philosophy**: This approach emphasizes serving others, focusing on team members' growth, and promoting a collaborative and ethical work environment.

- **Application to Risk Management**: As a servant leader, focus on empowering team members to take ownership of risk management processes, encouraging open communication, and supporting their development in risk management skills.

Coaching on Technical Aspects of Risk Management

1. Risk Identification and Analysis:

- Teach the team how to identify potential risks using tools like brainstorming, SWOT analysis, and checklists.

- Guide them in analyzing risks in terms of likelihood and impact.

2. Risk Response Planning:

- Coach on developing effective risk response strategies tailored to different types of risks.

- Encourage creativity in finding solutions and contingency plans.

3. Risk Monitoring and Control:

- Instruct on setting up monitoring systems to track risk triggers and the effectiveness of risk responses.
- Mentor on how to adjust risk management plans based on monitoring outcomes.

Fostering a Risk-Aware Culture

- **Encourage Open Communication**: Create an environment where team members feel comfortable discussing risks and uncertainties openly.
- **Promote Learning from Mistakes**: Encourage the team to view mistakes as learning opportunities, focusing on what can be improved rather than assigning blame.

Developing Skills and Empowerment

- **Training Opportunities**: Provide training sessions, workshops, and resources on risk management best practices.
- **Empower Decision-Making**: Empower team members to make decisions related to risk management, supporting them to take calculated risks.

Leading by Example

- **Model Risk Management Behaviors**: Demonstrate effective risk management in your actions and decision-making processes.
- **Share Experiences**: Share your experiences and lessons learned from past projects to provide practical insights.

Continuous Improvement

- **Feedback and Reflection**: Regularly seek and provide feedback on risk management activities. Reflect on what works well and what can be improved.
- **Stay Informed**: Keep the team updated on the latest trends and tools in risk management.

Conclusion

Coaching and mentoring on risk management best practices as a servant leader involves a balance between guiding the team in technical risk management skills and fostering a supportive and collaborative environment. It's about empowering the team to take ownership of risks, encouraging open dialogue, and focusing on continuous learning and improvement in risk management practices.

LEADERSHIP IN STAKEHOLDER ADOPTION OF RISK STRATEGY

Leading stakeholders to adopt the risk strategy is a crucial aspect of effective risk management. It involves not only presenting and explaining the strategy but also ensuring stakeholder buy-in and commitment. This process requires clear communication, understanding of stakeholder perspectives, and the ability to align the risk strategy with the overall project and organizational goals. Here's a structured approach:

Understanding Stakeholder Perspectives

1. **Identify Stakeholder Interests**: Understand what each stakeholder values and fears in the context of the project. Recognize their individual goals, concerns, and motivations.

2. **Assess Risk Tolerance**: Evaluate the risk tolerance levels of various stakeholders, as this will influence their acceptance of the risk strategy.

Effective Communication

1. **Clear Presentation**: Present the risk strategy in a clear, concise manner. Use language and concepts that are accessible to all stakeholders.

2. **Highlight Benefits**: Explain how the risk strategy aligns with the project objectives and benefits the stakeholders. Show how it addresses their concerns and adds value.

Engaging Stakeholders

1. **Inclusive Discussions**: Involve stakeholders in discussions about the risk strategy. Encourage them to express their views and concerns.

2. **Feedback Incorporation**: Be open to feedback and willing to adjust the strategy to accommodate reasonable stakeholder concerns and suggestions.

Alignment with Organizational and Project Goals

1. **Strategic Alignment**: Demonstrate how the risk strategy aligns with the broader organizational goals and the specific objectives of the project.

2. **Illustrate with Examples**: Use real-life examples or case studies to illustrate how effective risk management has benefited similar projects or organizations.

Alexander Stratton

Building Trust and Credibility

1. **Trust Building**: Establish trust through transparency, consistency in actions, and demonstrating a track record of successful risk management.

2. **Expertise and Knowledge**: Showcase your expertise and knowledge in risk management, reinforcing the credibility of the proposed strategy.

Gaining Commitment

1. **Shared Responsibility**: Emphasize the role of each stakeholder in implementing the risk strategy, fostering a sense of shared responsibility.

2. **Formal Agreements**: Where appropriate, formalize stakeholder commitment through agreements or documented endorsements.

Providing Support and Resources

1. **Training and Resources**: Offer training sessions and resources to help stakeholders understand and implement the risk strategy.

2. **Ongoing Support**: Provide ongoing support to stakeholders, addressing any challenges they face in adopting the strategy.

Regular Reviews and Adaptation

1. **Monitor and Review**: Regularly monitor the implementation of the risk strategy and its effectiveness.

2. **Adapt and Update**: Be prepared to adapt the strategy in response to changes in the project environment or stakeholder feedback.

Conclusion

Leading stakeholders to adopt a risk strategy requires a combination of effective communication, stakeholder engagement, alignment with goals, and building trust. It's about creating a shared understanding and commitment to the risk strategy, ensuring that it's seen as integral to the project's success. Regular monitoring, adaptation, and support are key to maintaining stakeholder engagement and commitment to the risk strategy over the life of the project.

CASE STUDY: PHARMACEUTICAL RESEARCH AND DEVELOPMENT PROJECT

Context

A global pharmaceutical company is initiating a high-stakes research and development project to develop a new drug. Given the complexity and potential risks associated with such projects, establishing a comprehensive risk management strategy is critical.

Establishing Risk Processes and Tools

- **Risk Assessment Framework:** Implementing a robust framework to identify, assess, and prioritize risks.

- **Risk Management Software:** Utilizing specialized software to track, monitor, and report risks throughout the project lifecycle.

- **Risk Reporting System:** Setting up a system for regular risk reporting, including dashboards and real-time alerts.

Providing Risk Management Templates/Forms

- **Risk Register Template:** Designing a template to document identified risks, their impacts, likelihood, and mitigation strategies.

- **Risk Analysis Matrix:** Creating a matrix to categorize risks based on their severity and probability.

- **Risk Response Plan:** Developing a template for documenting planned responses to various risk scenarios.

Determining Risk Metrics

- **Quantitative Metrics:** Such as potential financial impact, likelihood of occurrence, and expected value of risks.

- **Qualitative Metrics:** Including risk severity, stakeholder impact, and risk velocity (how quickly a risk could impact the project).

Identifying Risk Categories

- **Clinical Risks:** Related to patient safety, drug efficacy, and clinical trial outcomes.

- **Regulatory Risks:** Compliance with health regulations and standards across different regions.

- **Operational Risks:** Inefficiencies in research processes, resource allocation, and technology.

- **Market Risks:** Changes in market demand, competition, and pricing pressures.

Coaching/Mentoring Team on Risk Management Best Practices

- **Training Sessions:** Conducting workshops and training sessions on risk management methodologies and tools.

- **Servant Leadership:** Adopting a servant leadership approach, focusing on supporting and empowering the team to manage risks effectively.

- **Regular Consultations:** Providing ongoing support and guidance to the team on risk management issues.

Leading Stakeholders to Adopt the Risk Strategy

- **Stakeholder Engagement:** Regularly engaging with key stakeholders, including research teams, regulatory bodies, and investors, to communicate the risk management strategy.

- **Customized Presentations:** Tailoring presentations to different stakeholder groups to highlight relevant aspects of the risk management strategy.

- **Feedback Mechanism:** Establishing channels for stakeholders to provide feedback and input on the risk management process.

Conclusion

In this pharmaceutical R&D project, establishing a risk management strategy involves setting up structured processes, tools, and templates to systematically manage risks. Determining appropriate risk metrics and identifying specific risk categories pertinent to the pharmaceutical industry are crucial steps. By coaching the team in risk management best practices and leading stakeholders to adopt the risk strategy, the project risk manager ensures that all parties are aligned and equipped to handle potential risks effectively. This approach not only aligns with PMI standards but also ensures the project is managed proactively, increasing the likelihood of successful drug development and regulatory approval.

Task 5 Document the risk management plan

DEFINING ORGANIZATIONAL RISK ROLES AND RESPONSIBILITIES IN ALIGNMENT WITH PROJECT RAM

Defining organizational risk roles and responsibilities is a critical component of documenting the risk management plan. This involves clarifying who is accountable for managing specific risks and the various tasks associated with risk management. Aligning these roles and responsibilities with a project Responsibility Assignment Matrix (RAM), such as a RACI chart, further clarifies each team member's involvement in risk-related activities. Here's how to approach this:

1. Identify Key Risk Management Roles

- **Risk Owner**: Individuals responsible for managing specific risks and implementing response strategies.

- **Risk Management Team/Officer**: Group or individual tasked with overseeing the risk management process.

- **Project Manager**: Responsible for integrating risk management into overall project management activities.

- **Executive Sponsor**: Senior-level stakeholder providing oversight and support for the risk management process.

2. Define Specific Responsibilities

- **Risk Identification**: Assign who will identify risks (e.g., all team members, specific departments).

- **Risk Analysis**: Determine who will conduct qualitative and quantitative risk analyses.

- **Risk Response Planning**: Specify who is responsible for developing and implementing risk response plans.

- **Risk Monitoring**: Assign the task of tracking identified risks and the effectiveness of responses.

3. Use a RACI Chart for Alignment

- **Responsible (R)**: Those who do the work to complete the task. E.g., Project team members identifying potential risks.

- **Accountable (A)**: The individual who is ultimately accountable and has the final say. E.g., Project Manager or Risk Owner signing off the risk management plan.

- **Consulted (C)**: People or stakeholders who need to provide input before the work can be done and the decision made. E.g., Subject matter experts providing risk analysis input.

- **Informed (I)**: Those who need to be kept informed of progress or decisions, but do not directly contribute to the task. E.g., Executive Sponsors or higher management.

4. Integrate RAM with Risk Management Plan

- **Documentation**: Include the RACI chart or equivalent RAM in the risk management plan documentation.

- **Communication**: Ensure all stakeholders are aware of their roles and responsibilities as outlined in the RAM.

- **Alignment with Project Activities**: Align risk management roles and responsibilities with other project activities for a cohesive approach.

5. Regular Updates and Reviews

- **Review and Adjust**: Regularly review and adjust the roles and responsibilities as the project evolves and new risks emerge.

- **Feedback Mechanisms**: Establish feedback mechanisms to assess the effectiveness of the role assignments and make necessary adjustments.

Conclusion

Defining and aligning organizational risk roles and responsibilities with a project RAM like a RACI chart ensures clarity and efficiency in the risk management process. It delineates clear lines of accountability and involvement, reducing confusion and ensuring that all aspects of risk management are adequately addressed. Regular reviews and adjustments to these roles and responsibilities are essential to adapt to changing project dynamics and risk profiles.

COMPILATION OF KEY ARTIFACTS AND RESOURCES FOR THE RISK MANAGEMENT PLAN

Preparing a list of key artifacts and resources for compiling a risk management plan involves identifying and gathering various documents and tools that provide the necessary information and support for effective risk management. These artifacts and resources are critical in ensuring that the risk management plan is comprehensive, accurate, and aligned with the project's objectives. Here's a structured list of such key items:

1. Project Charter

- **Purpose**: Provides an overview of the project, including objectives, scope, key stakeholders, and high-level risks.

- **Use in Risk Management**: Serves as a foundational document for understanding the project's baseline for risk assessment.

2. Stakeholder Register

- **Purpose**: Lists all project stakeholders, their roles, interests, and potential impact on the project.

- **Use in Risk Management**: Essential for identifying stakeholder-related risks and for planning stakeholder engagement in risk management.

3. Project Management Plan

- **Purpose**: Includes detailed planning information covering scope, schedule, cost, quality, resources, and communications.

- **Use in Risk Management**: Provides comprehensive project details that are crucial for identifying and managing risks in various project areas.

4. Risk Management Policy

- **Purpose**: Outlines the organization's approach to risk management, including methodologies, tools, and techniques.

- **Use in Risk Management**: Guides the development of the risk management plan in line with organizational standards.

5. Risk Register Template

- **Purpose**: A tool for documenting identified risks, including their analysis, response plans, and monitoring status.

- **Use in Risk Management**: Central to tracking and managing risks throughout the project lifecycle.

6. Historical Data and Lessons Learned

- **Purpose**: Provides insights from previous projects, including successful risk management strategies and past mistakes.

- **Use in Risk Management**: Valuable for informing current risk planning and avoiding repeat issues.

7. Industry Benchmarks and Standards

- **Purpose**: Includes industry-specific risk management standards and benchmarks.

- **Use in Risk Management**: Helps in aligning the risk management plan with industry best practices.

8. Risk Analysis Tools and Software

- **Purpose**: Software and tools for qualitative and quantitative risk analysis (e.g., Monte Carlo simulations, risk assessment matrix).

- **Use in Risk Management**: Facilitates detailed risk analysis and prioritization.

9. Risk Response Plan Templates

- **Purpose**: Standardized templates for developing risk response strategies.

- **Use in Risk Management**: Ensures consistency and completeness in planning risk responses.

10. Communication Plan Template

- **Purpose**: Framework for planning how risk information will be communicated to stakeholders.

- **Use in Risk Management**: Crucial for ensuring effective and timely communication about risks.

11. Resource Allocation Documents

- **Purpose**: Details on resource allocation, including budget, personnel, and materials.

- **Use in Risk Management**: Important for assessing risks related to resource constraints and planning.

Conclusion

These artifacts and resources form the backbone of the risk management plan, providing necessary information and frameworks for risk identification, analysis, response planning, and monitoring. Their careful selection and use ensure a structured and thorough approach to risk management, aligned with both project-specific needs and organizational practices.

OUTLINING ESSENTIAL RISK MANAGEMENT ACTIVITIES

Outlining key risk management activities involves detailing the who, what, when, where, and how of each step in the risk management process. This structured approach ensures that all aspects of risk management are thoroughly addressed and integrated into the project lifecycle. Here's an outline of these key activities:

1. Risk Identification

- **Who**: Project team members, stakeholders, risk management team.

- **What**: Identify potential risks that could impact the project.

- **When**: Initially during the planning phase and then continuously throughout the project lifecycle.

- **Where**: Conducted during team meetings, workshops, and through ongoing project activities.

- **How**: Using techniques like brainstorming, SWOT analysis, expert interviews, and reviewing historical data and lessons learned.

2. Risk Analysis

- **Who**: Risk analysts, project managers, subject matter experts.

- **What**: Assess the identified risks to determine their likelihood and potential impact.

- **When**: Following risk identification and periodically as project conditions change.

- **Where**: Utilizing data and insights gathered from project documents and stakeholder inputs.

- **How**: Through qualitative methods (like risk probability and impact matrix) and quantitative methods (such as Monte Carlo simulations).

3. Risk Prioritization

- **Who**: Project manager, risk management team, key stakeholders.

- **What**: Prioritize risks based on their analysis to focus on the most critical risks.

- **When**: After risk analysis and as part of regular project review meetings.

- **Where**: Integrated into regular project management and planning sessions.

- **How**: Using tools like a risk matrix to rank risks by their severity.

4. Risk Response Planning

- **Who**: Project manager, risk owners, project team members.

- **What**: Develop strategies to address each significant risk (avoid, mitigate, transfer, accept).

- **When**: As soon as significant risks are identified and analyzed.

- **Where**: Within the framework of the overall project management plan.

- **How**: By assigning risk owners and outlining specific action plans for each risk.

5. Risk Monitoring and Control

- **Who**: Risk owners, project manager, project team.
- **What**: Continuously monitor risks and the effectiveness of risk responses.
- **When**: Throughout the project lifecycle.
- **Where**: Across all project activities and processes.
- **How**: Through regular risk reviews, tracking risk triggers, and adjusting risk plans as needed.

6. Risk Communication

- **Who**: Project manager, risk management team, all project stakeholders.
- **What**: Communicate risk information, updates, and changes to all relevant parties.
- **When**: At regular intervals and as significant risks or responses change.
- **Where**: Via project meetings, reports, and communication channels like emails or project management tools.
- **How**: Using a structured communication plan that specifies what information is communicated, to whom, when, and through which channels.

7. Risk Documentation and Reporting

- **Who**: Project manager, risk management team.
- **What**: Document risk management activities and report to stakeholders.
- **When**: Throughout the project, with specific reports at key milestones.
- **Where**: In the project's central documentation repository.
- **How**: Through standardized templates and reports, ensuring documentation is accessible and comprehensible.

Conclusion

These key risk management activities form a comprehensive approach to managing project risks. By clearly defining who is involved, what needs to be done, when and where each activity should take place, and how to execute each step, you create a robust framework for effective risk management throughout the project lifecycle. Regular reviews and updates to these activities ensure that the risk management process remains dynamic and responsive to changing project conditions.

UTILIZATION OF RISK BREAKDOWN STRUCTURE (RBS) IN SUPPORTING THE RISK MANAGEMENT PLAN

The Risk Breakdown Structure (RBS) is a fundamental tool in risk management, serving as a hierarchical decomposition of risks that might impact a project. It is used to categorize and organize risks, facilitating a systematic approach to risk identification, analysis, and management. Here's how the RBS can be utilized to support the risk management plan:

1. Facilitating Comprehensive Risk Identification

- **Structured Framework**: RBS provides a structured framework that helps in identifying risks across various categories systematically.

- **Categories and Subcategories**: It breaks down risks into categories and subcategories, ensuring that all potential areas of risk are explored. For example, categories can include technical risks, financial risks, operational risks, etc.

2. Enhancing Understanding of Risk Interrelationships

- **Visual Representation**: The hierarchical nature of RBS allows for a visual representation of risks, highlighting how different risks are related or interconnected.

- **Depth of Analysis**: By breaking down risks into finer details, RBS enables a more in-depth analysis of each risk and its components.

3. Aiding in Risk Prioritization and Response

- **Prioritization**: RBS helps in categorizing risks by their significance or impact level, aiding in prioritizing which risks need more immediate attention or robust response strategies.

- **Targeted Responses**: By understanding the specific category a risk falls into, more targeted and effective risk response strategies can be developed.

4. Resource Allocation

- **Focused Resources**: RBS enables project managers to allocate resources more effectively by identifying which areas of the project carry more risk and therefore may require more resources.

- **Budgeting**: It also assists in budgeting for risk management activities by providing insights into the potential impact and resource requirements of different risk categories.

5. Communication and Reporting

- **Stakeholder Communication**: RBS serves as a tool for communicating risks to stakeholders in an organized manner, making it easier to understand the breadth and depth of potential project risks.

- **Standardized Reporting**: It provides a standard format for reporting risks, ensuring consistency in how risk information is conveyed and understood.

6. Continuous Risk Monitoring

- **Monitoring Framework**: The RBS structure allows for continuous monitoring and updating of risks as the project progresses, ensuring that new risks are identified and categorized appropriately.

- **Feedback Loop**: It creates a feedback loop where information from ongoing risk monitoring can be used to update and refine the RBS.

Conclusion

The Risk Breakdown Structure is an invaluable tool in the risk management process. It supports the risk management plan by providing a clear, structured approach to risk identification, analysis, prioritization, and response. The RBS ensures that risks are managed in an organized, methodical manner, aligning closely with the overall objectives and structure of the project management plan.

DEVELOPMENT OF A COMPREHENSIVE RISK COMMUNICATION PLAN

Defining a risk communication plan is an essential element of the risk management process. A risk communication plan outlines how risk information will be disseminated among project stakeholders. It ensures that everyone involved in the project is informed about the risks and understands their impact and the measures being taken to manage them. Here's a guide to defining a comprehensive risk communication plan:

1. Identifying Stakeholders

- **List Stakeholders**: Identify all stakeholders who need to be informed about project risks. This includes the project team, management, clients, suppliers, and any other relevant parties.

- **Understand Information Needs**: Determine the type and level of risk information relevant to each stakeholder group.

2. Determining the What, When, and How

- **What to Communicate**: Decide on the risk information that needs to be communicated. This includes details about identified risks, their potential impact, response strategies, and any changes in risk status.

- **When to Communicate**: Establish the frequency of communication. This could be on a regular schedule (e.g., weekly, monthly) or as risks are identified and resolved.

- **How to Communicate**: Choose the methods of communication, which could include email updates, regular meetings, reports, dashboards, or real-time alerts for critical risks.

3. Assigning Responsibilities

- **Communicators**: Assign who will be responsible for communicating risk information. Typically, this is the project manager or risk manager, but other team members might also be involved.

- **Feedback Channels**: Designate channels through which stakeholders can provide feedback or seek clarification.

4. Developing Messaging Strategies

- **Tailoring Messages**: Develop messaging strategies tailored to the needs and understanding of different stakeholders.

- **Clarity and Transparency**: Ensure that communication is clear, concise, and transparent, avoiding technical jargon where possible.

5. Establishing Communication Protocols

- **Standard Procedures**: Establish standard procedures for risk communication, including templates and guidelines for reporting risks.

- **Escalation Processes**: Define escalation processes for high-risk situations where immediate attention is required.

6. Training and Support

- **Training Stakeholders**: Provide training to stakeholders on how to interpret and act on risk information.

- **Support Channels**: Set up support channels for stakeholders who need assistance or additional information.

7. Monitoring and Adjustments

- **Feedback and Evaluation**: Regularly gather feedback on the effectiveness of the communication plan and make adjustments as needed.

- **Adaptability**: Be prepared to adapt the communication strategy in response to project changes or stakeholder feedback.

8. Documentation and Record Keeping

- **Documentation**: Document all communications related to risks for accountability and future reference.

- **Record Keeping**: Maintain records of how risk communications were handled, including stakeholder responses and outcomes.

Conclusion

A well-defined risk communication plan is critical for ensuring that all stakeholders are kept informed about risks and are able to respond appropriately. Effective communication enhances the overall risk management process, supports stakeholder engagement, and contributes to the success of the project.

ESTABLISHMENT OF RISK PRIORITIZATION CRITERIA

Defining risk prioritization criteria is a key aspect of effective risk management. This process involves establishing the parameters for evaluating and ranking risks, ensuring that the most significant risks are identified and addressed first. Effective risk prioritization allows for the optimal allocation of resources and focused risk response strategies. Here's a guide to defining risk prioritization criteria:

1. Probability of Occurrence

- **Definition**: Assess how likely it is that each risk will occur.

- **Scale**: Develop a scale (e.g., high, medium, low) or a percentage likelihood to quantify probability.

2. Impact on Project Objectives

- **Scope of Impact**: Evaluate the potential impact of each risk on key project objectives such as scope, schedule, cost, and quality.

- **Severity Levels**: Establish severity levels for impacts (e.g., critical, major, minor) to categorize the potential consequences.

3. Risk Velocity

- **Definition**: Assess how quickly a risk could impact the project once it occurs.

- **Consideration**: Prioritize risks that have a rapid impact, as they may require more immediate attention.

4. Risk Exposure

- **Calculation**: Combine the probability and impact to calculate the overall risk exposure. This can be done using a risk matrix.

- **Ranking**: Use the risk exposure value to rank and prioritize risks.

5. Resource Availability

- **Resource Constraints**: Consider the availability and constraints of resources (financial, human, technical) required to manage each risk.

- **Prioritization**: Prioritize risks where the necessary resources are scarce or expensive.

6. Stakeholder Tolerance and Concern

- **Stakeholder Impact**: Assess how each risk aligns with stakeholder concerns and their tolerance levels.

- **Engagement**: Prioritize risks that are of high concern to key stakeholders to maintain their support and confidence.

7. Risk Dependencies and Interactions

- **Interrelated Risks**: Identify risks that are dependent on each other or have a cascading effect.

- **Cumulative Impact**: Prioritize risks based on their cumulative impact due to dependencies and interactions.

8. Regulatory and Compliance Factors

- **Legal Implications**: Consider the risks associated with regulatory and compliance requirements.

- **Priority**: Give higher priority to risks that could lead to legal or compliance issues.

9. Strategic Alignment

- **Alignment with Goals**: Evaluate how each risk aligns with the strategic goals and objectives of the project and the organization.

- **Prioritization**: Prioritize risks that could significantly derail strategic outcomes.

Conclusion

The criteria for risk prioritization should be tailored to the specific context of the project and the organization. It's important to use a combination of these criteria to get a holistic view of each risk's significance. Regular reviews and adjustments of the prioritization criteria are necessary as project conditions and external environments change. Effective risk prioritization ensures that the most critical risks are managed proactively, enhancing the likelihood of project success.

FORMULATION OF STAKEHOLDER EMPOWERMENT AND EDUCATION STRATEGY

Defining a stakeholder empowerment and education strategy is crucial in risk management, as it ensures that all stakeholders are knowledgeable about risk processes and feel empowered to contribute effectively to risk management activities. This strategy involves creating opportunities for learning, fostering a culture of open communication, and actively involving stakeholders in risk management decisions. Here's a structured approach to defining this strategy:

1. Identification of Stakeholder Groups

- **Categorize Stakeholders**: Identify different groups of stakeholders based on their role, influence, and level of involvement in the project.

- **Assess Needs**: Understand the specific risk management knowledge needs and preferences of each stakeholder group.

2. Educational Programs and Training

- **Tailored Training Sessions**: Develop training sessions tailored to the varying levels of expertise and roles of stakeholders. This can include workshops, webinars, and e-learning courses.

- **Focus Areas**: Cover key risk management concepts, processes, tools, and their application in the project context.

3. Communication and Information Sharing

- **Regular Updates**: Provide regular and clear updates on risk management activities, including identified risks, their status, and actions taken.

- **Two-way Communication Channels**: Establish channels for stakeholders to ask questions, provide feedback, and share their insights.

4. Involvement in Risk Management Activities

- **Participation in Risk Identification**: Involve stakeholders in identifying risks, leveraging their unique perspectives and knowledge.

- **Collaborative Decision-Making**: Engage stakeholders in decision making processes related to risk responses and mitigation strategies.

5. Creating a Culture of Risk Awareness

- **Promote Risk Awareness**: Foster a culture where risk awareness is integrated into daily activities and decision-making processes.

- **Encourage Proactive Behavior**: Encourage stakeholders to proactively identify and report risks, and to suggest improvements.

6. Empowerment through Responsibility and Authority

- **Assign Risk-Related Roles**: Assign specific risk-related roles and responsibilities to stakeholders, empowering them to take an active part in risk management.

- **Provide Necessary Authority**: Ensure stakeholders have the authority to make decisions and take actions within their assigned risk-related roles.

7. Supportive Resources and Tools

- **Access to Resources**: Provide stakeholders with access to risk management resources, tools, and documentation.

- **Guidance and Support**: Offer ongoing support and guidance in risk management practices, including access to risk management experts.

8. Feedback Mechanism and Continuous Improvement

- **Feedback Loops**: Implement mechanisms for stakeholders to provide feedback on the risk management process and their training needs.

- **Continuous Learning**: Regularly review and update training programs and strategies based on stakeholder feedback and evolving project requirements.

Conclusion

A well-defined stakeholder empowerment and education strategy in risk management is key to ensuring that all stakeholders are informed, skilled, and actively involved in managing risks. By focusing on tailored education, open communication, collaborative involvement, and fostering a proactive risk culture, stakeholders become more empowered to contribute effectively to the project's success. Continuous feedback and improvement of this strategy are essential to adapt to changing needs and project dynamics.

CASE STUDY: AIRPORT EXPANSION PROJECT

Context

A major airport is undergoing an expansion project, which includes the construction of new terminals and runways. Documenting the risk management plan is a crucial step in ensuring that the project is completed on time, within budget, and to the required standards.

Defining Organizational Risk Roles and Responsibilities

- **Organizational Risk Roles:** Identifying key roles such as Project Risk Manager, Risk Analyst, and various project team leaders.

- **Responsibilities Alignment:** Utilizing a Responsibility Assignment Matrix (RAM), specifically a RACI chart (Responsible, Accountable, Consulted, Informed) to clarify the roles and responsibilities of each team member in relation to risk management.

Preparing a List of Key Artifacts/Resources

- **Risk Management Policy:** The guiding document outlining the approach to risk management.

- **Risk Register:** A dynamic document listing all identified risks with their assessment and response strategies.

- **Risk Analysis Tools:** Software and tools used for risk identification and analysis, like Monte Carlo simulations or decision tree analysis.

Outlining Key Risk Management Activities

- **Who:** Assigning specific team members or departments to each risk management activity.

- **What:** Detailed description of each activity, such as risk identification, assessment, response planning, and monitoring.

- **When:** Timeline for each activity, including frequency of risk assessments and reviews.

- **Where:** Location of meetings, storage of documents, and platforms used for communication.

- **How:** Methodologies and tools to be used for each risk management activity.

Utilizing the Risk Breakdown Structure (RBS)

- **Explanation:** RBS is a hierarchical representation of risks, categorized by source or nature, which aids in systematic identification and management of risks.

- **Support for Plan:** Using RBS to ensure comprehensive risk identification and categorization, aligning with the project's scope and objectives.

Defining a Risk Communication Plan

- **Channels of Communication:** Establishing regular meetings, reports, and digital communication channels.

- **Frequency and Format:** Scheduling the frequency of risk updates and the format in which they will be communicated.

- **Target Audience:** Tailoring the communication content and style to different stakeholder groups.

Defining Risk Prioritization Criteria

- **Criteria:** Establishing criteria based on the impact, probability, and urgency of risks.

- **Prioritization Process:** A clear process for evaluating and prioritizing risks, ensuring the most critical risks are addressed first.

Defining Stakeholder Empowerment and Education Strategy

- **Empowerment:** Involving stakeholders in risk management processes to enhance their understanding and buy-in.

- **Education:** Conducting training sessions and workshops to educate stakeholders about risk management principles and practices.

Conclusion

For the airport expansion project, documenting the risk management plan involves a comprehensive approach, starting from defining roles and responsibilities using a RACI chart to outlining the key activities and tools involved in risk management. The use of RBS helps in structuring risk identification and categorization, while a well-defined risk communication plan ensures that all stakeholders are kept informed and engaged. Establishing clear risk prioritization criteria and a strategy for stakeholder empowerment and education are essential to ensure that the risk management plan is effective and widely accepted. This structured documentation aligns with PMI standards and provides a robust foundation for managing the complex risks associated with a large-scale infrastructure project.

Task 6 Plan and lead risk management activities with stakeholders

COLLABORATION WITH THE TEAM FOR RISK PLANNING IN PROJECTS

Collaborating with the team that would conduct risk planning on a project is a critical aspect of Task 6 in risk management. This collaboration involves coordinating with various team members who have different roles, expertise, and perspectives on risk. Effective collaboration ensures that the risk planning process is comprehensive, inclusive, and leverages the collective knowledge and skills of the team. Here's how to approach this collaboration:

1. Assemble the Risk Planning Team

- **Team Composition**: Identify and bring together individuals who will be part of the risk planning process. This team should include project managers, risk management specialists, key project team members, and representatives from critical stakeholder groups.

- **Diverse Expertise**: Ensure the team has diverse expertise, including technical knowledge, project management experience, and an understanding of the business environment.

2. Define Roles and Responsibilities

- **Clarity of Roles**: Clearly define and communicate the roles and responsibilities of each team member in the risk planning process. This might include who will lead the identification of risks, who will analyze them, who will develop response strategies, etc.

- **Leverage Strengths**: Assign roles based on each team member's strengths and areas of expertise.

3. Establish Risk Planning Objectives

- **Shared Goals**: Set clear objectives for the risk planning process. Ensure that these objectives align with the overall project goals and risk management policy of the organization.

- **Success Criteria**: Define what success looks like for the risk planning process. This could include specific milestones or deliverables.

4. Facilitate Effective Communication

- **Regular Meetings**: Schedule regular meetings to discuss risk planning activities, share insights, and track progress.

- **Open Communication Channels**: Establish open lines of communication among team members for ongoing dialogue and information sharing.

5. Encourage Collaboration and Input

- **Inclusive Discussions**: Foster an environment where all team members feel comfortable sharing their ideas and concerns.

- **Brainstorming Sessions**: Conduct brainstorming sessions to collectively identify potential risks.

6. Utilize Collaborative Tools

- **Project Management Software**: Use project management software tools that facilitate collaboration, such as shared workspaces, document sharing, and collaborative risk registers.

- **Visualization Tools**: Employ visualization tools like flowcharts or mind maps to help in understanding and discussing risks.

7. Knowledge Sharing and Learning

- **Shared Learning**: Encourage team members to share their knowledge and experiences related to risk management.

- **Training Sessions**: Organize training sessions if needed to ensure all team members have the necessary knowledge and skills for risk planning.

8. Monitoring and Feedback

- **Track Progress**: Regularly monitor the progress of the risk planning activities and make adjustments as necessary.

- **Feedback Loop**: Implement a feedback loop to continually improve the collaboration process based on team members' experiences and suggestions.

Conclusion

Effective collaboration in risk planning involves bringing together a diverse team, defining clear roles and objectives, facilitating open communication, and fostering an inclusive environment for idea sharing. By leveraging the collective expertise and insights of the team, the risk planning process becomes more robust and aligned with the project's needs and goals. Regular monitoring and feedback ensure that this collaborative approach remains dynamic and responsive to the project's evolving context.

UTILIZATION OF STAKEHOLDER ANALYSIS CONDUCTED BY THE PROJECT MANAGER

Leveraging stakeholder analysis done by the project manager is a crucial step in risk management, especially in Task 6, which focuses on planning and leading risk management activities with stakeholders. The stakeholder analysis provides valuable insights into the interests, influence, and impact of various stakeholders on the project, which can significantly affect the risk management process. Here's how to effectively leverage this analysis:

1. Understanding Stakeholder Dynamics

- **Review the Stakeholder Analysis**: Start by thoroughly reviewing the stakeholder analysis document. Understand who the key stakeholders are, their roles, interests, influence levels, and attitudes towards risk.

- **Identify Stakeholder Relationships**: Assess how stakeholders relate to each other and to the project. This can reveal potential sources of conflict or cooperation that might impact risk management.

2. Aligning Risk Management with Stakeholder Interests

- **Tailor Risk Strategies**: Develop risk management strategies that align with the interests and concerns of key stakeholders. This ensures that risk responses are more likely to be supported and effectively implemented.

- **Addressing Concerns**: Use the analysis to proactively address stakeholder concerns about risks, which can help in gaining their buy-in for the risk management plan.

3. Engaging Stakeholders Based on Their Influence

- **High-Influence Stakeholders**: Prioritize engagement with stakeholders who have significant influence over the project. Their support can be crucial in implementing effective risk responses.

- **Communication Strategy**: Develop a communication strategy that reflects the level of influence and interest of each stakeholder group.

4. Utilizing Stakeholders' Knowledge and Expertise

- **Risk Identification**: Involve stakeholders in identifying risks, leveraging their knowledge and insights about different aspects of the project.

- **Expert Consultation**: Consult with technical experts or high-impact stakeholders for detailed risk analysis and development of mitigation strategies.

5. Managing Stakeholder Expectations

- **Set Realistic Expectations**: Use the stakeholder analysis to understand and manage expectations regarding the project's risk management capabilities.

- **Feedback and Adaptation**: Regularly solicit feedback from stakeholders and adapt risk management plans according to their inputs and changing project dynamics.

6. Integrating Stakeholder Analysis in Risk Documentation

- **Update Risk Register**: Incorporate information from the stakeholder analysis into the risk register, especially regarding risk ownership and stakeholder-related risks.

- **Documenting Stakeholder Engagement**: Keep a record of how stakeholder analysis is used to inform risk management decisions and stakeholder engagement activities.

Conclusion

Effectively leveraging stakeholder analysis in risk management involves understanding the stakeholders' attributes and dynamics, aligning risk strategies with their interests, engaging them based on their influence, and utilizing their knowledge. This approach ensures that risk management activities are informed, inclusive, and have the necessary support from key stakeholders, thereby enhancing the overall effectiveness of the project's risk management efforts. Regular updates and adaptations to stakeholder analysis are crucial to maintain its relevance throughout the project lifecycle.

MANAGEMENT OF STAKEHOLDER RISK APPETITE AND ATTITUDES

Managing stakeholder risk appetite and attitudes is a critical aspect of risk management, particularly in Task 6, which involves planning and leading risk management activities with stakeholders. Stakeholders' attitudes towards risk and their appetite for risk-taking can significantly influence the direction and effectiveness of risk management strategies. Here's how to approach this management task:

1. Understanding Stakeholder Risk Appetite

- **Assess Risk Tolerance**: Begin by assessing the risk tolerance of each stakeholder or stakeholder group. This involves understanding how much risk they are comfortable taking on in relation to the project.

- **Identify Variations**: Acknowledge that risk appetite can vary widely among stakeholders, depending on their role, experience, and vested interests in the project.

2. Evaluating Stakeholder Attitudes

- **Gather Insights**: Collect information on stakeholders' attitudes towards specific risks through meetings, surveys, or direct conversations.

- **Attitude Analysis**: Analyze whether stakeholders are generally risk-averse, risk-neutral, or risk-seeking, and understand the rationale behind these attitudes.

3. Aligning Risk Management with Risk Appetite

- **Tailor Risk Strategies**: Develop risk management strategies that align with the overall risk appetite of the key stakeholders. This ensures that the risk responses are acceptable and supported by them.

- **Balance Different Appetites**: Find a balance in risk management approaches to accommodate varying risk appetites, especially when they conflict.

4. Communicating About Risks

- **Open Dialogue**: Foster an environment where stakeholders can openly discuss their views and concerns about risks.

- **Educational Communication**: Use communication as a tool to educate stakeholders about risks, the potential impact on the project, and the rationale behind chosen risk strategies.

5. Influencing and Shaping Attitudes

- **Influence Through Information**: Provide stakeholders with detailed information and data to help shape their attitudes towards risks. Well-informed stakeholders are more likely to have a balanced view of risks.

- **Demonstrate Benefits**: Highlight the benefits of certain risk-taking within the boundaries of the project's objectives to positively influence risk-averse stakeholders.

6. Regular Reviews and Adaptations

- **Monitor Changes**: Regularly monitor any changes in stakeholder risk appetite and attitudes, as they can evolve over the course of the project.

- **Adapt Strategies**: Be prepared to adapt risk management strategies in response to significant shifts in stakeholder risk appetite or attitudes.

7. Documenting and Reporting

- **Record Keeping**: Document assessments of stakeholder risk appetite and attitudes, and how they have been factored into risk management planning.

- **Reporting**: Include information about stakeholder risk appetite and attitudes in regular risk management reports.

Conclusion

Effectively managing stakeholder risk appetite and attitudes involves a deep understanding of their perspectives, continuous communication, and the alignment of risk strategies with their tolerance levels. It's important to balance different appetites, influence attitudes positively, and adapt strategies as needed. This approach ensures that risk management activities are not only aligned with project objectives but also have the necessary buy-in and support from stakeholders.

ESTABLISHMENT OF CLEAR EXPECTATIONS WITH STAKEHOLDERS ON ENGAGEMENT RULES

Engaging stakeholders in the risk prioritization process is a crucial step in effective risk management. Stakeholders often have diverse insights, interests, and perspectives that can significantly contribute to a more comprehensive understanding and assessment of risks. Here's a structured approach to involve stakeholders in risk prioritization:

1. Identify and Segment Stakeholders

- **Categorize Stakeholders**: Identify which stakeholders should be involved in the risk prioritization process. This can include project team members, management, clients, and external partners.

- **Segmentation**: Segment stakeholders based on their influence, interest, and expertise related to the project's risks.

2. Communicate the Purpose and Process

- **Clarify Objectives**: Clearly communicate the objectives of risk prioritization and how it fits into the larger risk management plan.

- **Explain the Process**: Describe how risks will be assessed, including criteria for prioritization such as impact, likelihood, and urgency.

3. Solicit Input and Perspectives

- **Gather Risk Insights**: Encourage stakeholders to share their insights on potential risks, based on their experience and knowledge of the project.

- **Feedback Mechanisms**: Use surveys, interviews, or workshops to collect stakeholder input on risk identification and assessment.

4. Facilitate Collaborative Workshops

- **Risk Assessment Workshops**: Organize workshops where stakeholders can collaboratively assess and prioritize risks.

- **Guided Discussions**: Lead discussions that allow stakeholders to express their views on the severity and implications of identified risks.

5. Use Structured Prioritization Tools

- **Risk Matrix**: Utilize tools like a risk matrix to help stakeholders visualize and understand the relative priority of each risk.

- **Scoring Systems**: Implement a scoring system to quantify risk impact and likelihood, facilitating a more objective prioritization process.

6. Acknowledge Different Risk Perceptions

- **Balance Diverse Views**: Recognize and balance differing perceptions of risk among stakeholders. Some may be more risk-averse while others may be more willing to take risks.

- **Reconcile Conflicting Opinions**: Address and reconcile conflicting opinions on risk priorities, aiming for a consensus or a balanced approach.

7. Integrate Stakeholder Feedback

- **Consolidation of Inputs**: Integrate the collective inputs from stakeholders into the risk prioritization process.

- **Review and Adjustment**: Regularly review and adjust risk priorities based on ongoing stakeholder feedback and project developments.

8. Transparent Communication and Documentation

- **Feedback Loop**: Keep stakeholders informed about how their input has influenced risk prioritization.

- **Document Decisions**: Document the risk prioritization process and decisions made, including the rationale behind them.

Conclusion

Engaging stakeholders in the risk prioritization process helps in gaining diverse perspectives, increasing buy-in, and enhancing the accuracy of risk assessments. It's important to facilitate effective communication, use structured tools for assessment, and acknowledge varying risk perceptions. Keeping the process transparent and documenting decisions are essential for maintaining clarity and accountability.

CUSTOMIZATION OF RISK COMMUNICATION FOR DIFFERENT STAKEHOLDERS

Setting appropriate expectations with stakeholders on the rules of engagement is a critical component of effective stakeholder management and risk management. Clear rules of engagement outline how stakeholders will interact with the project, particularly in relation to risk management activities. These guidelines help in establishing a mutual understanding and a structured approach to collaboration and communication. Here's how to set these expectations:

1. Define the Scope of Engagement

- **Clarify Roles**: Clearly define what roles and responsibilities stakeholders have in the risk management process. This includes who will be involved in risk identification, analysis, decision-making, and response implementation.

- **Boundaries**: Set boundaries for stakeholder involvement, ensuring that their engagement is productive and relevant to their expertise and interests.

2. Communication Protocols

- **Channels and Tools**: Specify the channels and tools to be used for communication (e.g., meetings, emails, project management software).

- **Frequency and Format**: Establish how often communications will occur (e.g., regular meetings, updates) and in what format (written reports, dashboards, presentations).

3. Decision-Making Processes

- **Involvement in Decisions**: Outline how and to what extent stakeholders will be involved in decision-making processes, especially those related to risk responses.

- **Consensus vs. Command**: Define whether decisions will be made by consensus or if they will be command-based, with specific individuals having the final say.

4. Feedback Mechanisms

- **Providing Feedback**: Encourage and facilitate stakeholders to provide feedback on risk management activities.

- **Handling Feedback**: Explain how feedback will be collected, reviewed, and integrated into the project.

5. Conflict Resolution Protocols

- **Resolution Processes**: Establish a process for resolving conflicts, particularly those related to risk priorities or response strategies.

- **Neutral Arbitration**: Consider having a neutral party to arbitrate in cases of significant disagreement.

6. Expectations on Risk Reporting

- **Reporting Requirements**: Communicate what risk information stakeholders are expected to report, how, and to whom.

- **Transparency and Honesty**: Emphasize the importance of transparency and honesty in reporting risks.

7. Training and Resources

- **Educational Support**: Offer training and resources to stakeholders to ensure they understand the risk management process and their role in it.

- **Accessibility of Information**: Ensure that stakeholders have access to all the necessary information and resources needed to effectively engage in the project.

8. Regular Review and Adaptation

- **Adapting Engagement Rules**: Be open to adapting the rules of engagement as the project evolves and as stakeholders' needs and circumstances change.

- **Periodic Reviews**: Schedule periodic reviews of engagement effectiveness and make adjustments as needed.

Conclusion

Setting appropriate expectations with stakeholders on the rules of engagement is crucial for ensuring smooth collaboration and effective risk management. It involves clearly defining roles, communication protocols, decision-making processes, and feedback mechanisms. Regular review and adaptation of these expectations are essential to respond to changing project dynamics and stakeholder needs.

LEADERSHIP IN STAKEHOLDER EMPOWERMENT FOR IMPLEMENTING RISK STRATEGIES

Tailoring risk communication for stakeholders is a vital part of effective risk management. Different stakeholders have varied interests, levels of understanding, and concerns regarding project risks. Therefore, customizing the communication of risk information to meet the specific needs and preferences of each stakeholder group is essential. Here's how to approach tailoring risk communication:

1. Understand Stakeholder Profiles

- **Analyze Stakeholder Characteristics**: Assess the knowledge level, interest, influence, and risk tolerance of each stakeholder or stakeholder group.

- **Identify Communication Preferences**: Understand each stakeholder's preferred communication method, frequency, and level of detail.

2. Customize the Message

- **Relevance**: Ensure the risk information is relevant to the specific concerns and areas of interest of each stakeholder.

- **Complexity**: Adjust the complexity of the information based on the stakeholder's level of expertise and familiarity with risk concepts.

3. Choose Appropriate Communication Channels

- **Varied Channels**: Use different channels for different stakeholders based on their preferences. This can include emails, meetings, reports, dashboards, or briefings.

- **Accessibility**: Make sure the chosen channels are easily accessible to the stakeholders.

4. Frequency and Timing

- **Regular Updates**: Determine the frequency of risk communications – more frequent for high-impact stakeholders or less frequent for those less directly involved.

- **Timely Information**: Ensure that stakeholders receive risk information in a timely manner, especially when immediate actions or decisions are required.

5. Clarity and Transparency

- **Clear Language**: Use clear, concise language, avoiding technical jargon unless the stakeholders are familiar with it.

- **Transparency**: Be transparent about the nature, impact, and probability of risks, as well as about the uncertainty and limitations in information.

6. Incorporate Visual Aids

- **Use of Visuals**: Utilize visual aids like charts, graphs, and diagrams to help stakeholders understand complex risk information.

- **Customized Visuals**: Tailor these visuals to suit the information needs and comprehension level of each stakeholder group.

7. Feedback and Interaction

- **Encourage Feedback**: Invite stakeholders to ask questions, provide feedback, and express their concerns.

- **Interactive Communication**: Foster a two-way communication process where stakeholders can interact and discuss risk information.

8. Document and Record

- **Consistent Records**: Keep consistent records of all risk communications for transparency and future reference.

- **Documentation Format**: Adjust the format and detail of documentation according to stakeholder needs and requirements.

9. Review and Adapt

- **Evaluate Effectiveness**: Regularly review the effectiveness of the communication strategy and make adjustments based on stakeholder feedback and changing project dynamics.

Conclusion

Tailoring risk communication for stakeholders involves understanding their unique needs and preferences and adjusting the message, channel, frequency, and format of communication accordingly. This personalized approach ensures that stakeholders are adequately informed and engaged, leading to better risk management outcomes and stakeholder satisfaction. Regular reviews and adaptations of the communication strategy are essential to maintain its effectiveness throughout the project lifecycle.

TRAINING, COACHING, AND EDUCATING STAKEHOLDERS IN RISK MANAGEMENT PRINCIPLES AND PROCESSES

Leading stakeholder empowerment for risk strategies in the risk management plan involves engaging stakeholders actively in the risk management process and enabling them to contribute effectively. Empowered stakeholders can provide valuable insights, support risk decision-making, and help implement risk responses more efficiently. Here's a structured approach to leading this empowerment:

1. Stakeholder Identification and Analysis

- **Identify Key Stakeholders**: Determine who the key stakeholders are in relation to the project's risk management.

- **Understand Their Influence and Interest**: Analyze each stakeholder's level of influence and interest regarding the project's risks.

2. Clear Communication of Risk Management Goals

- **Articulate Objectives**: Clearly communicate the goals of the risk management plan, ensuring stakeholders understand the importance of their role.

- **Align With Stakeholder Interests**: Show how effective risk management aligns with stakeholders' interests and the overall success of the project.

3. Involvement in Risk Identification and Analysis

- **Solicit Input**: Encourage stakeholders to identify potential risks based on their knowledge and experience.

- **Collaborative Analysis**: Involve stakeholders in risk analysis to leverage their expertise in assessing risk likelihood and impact.

4. Training and Knowledge Sharing

- **Provide Training**: Offer training sessions to stakeholders on key risk management principles and practices.

- **Knowledge Sharing Platforms**: Create forums or platforms for stakeholders to share insights and learn from each other.

5. Delegation of Risk-Related Responsibilities

- **Assign Roles**: Delegate specific risk-related roles and responsibilities to stakeholders, such as risk monitoring or implementing particular risk responses.

- **Authority to Act**: Ensure stakeholders have the authority and resources needed to act on their assigned responsibilities effectively.

6. Encouraging Proactive Participation

- **Empower Decision Making**: Empower stakeholders to make or contribute to decisions regarding risk responses.

- **Recognition of Contributions**: Acknowledge and appreciate stakeholders' contributions to the risk management process.

7. Creating Feedback Loops

- **Regular Reviews**: Conduct regular review meetings with stakeholders to discuss the status of risks and risk management activities.

- **Feedback Mechanism**: Establish a mechanism for stakeholders to provide feedback on the risk management process and suggest improvements.

8. Adjusting Strategies Based on Stakeholder Input

- **Responsive to Change**: Be open to adjusting risk strategies based on stakeholder input and changing project dynamics.

- **Continuous Improvement**: Use stakeholder feedback for the continuous improvement of risk management practices.

9. Building a Risk-Aware Culture

- **Promote Risk Awareness**: Foster a culture where risk awareness is part of the everyday mindset.

- **Encourage Open Dialogue**: Create an environment where discussing risks and uncertainties is encouraged and valued.

Conclusion

Empowering stakeholders in the risk management plan is about actively involving them in the process, providing them with the necessary knowledge and authority, and valuing their contributions. This approach not only enhances the effectiveness of the risk management plan but also promotes a sense of ownership and commitment among stakeholders, leading to better risk management outcomes Regular communication, training, and feedback are key to maintaining this empowerment throughout the project.

CASE STUDY: IT SYSTEM UPGRADE IN A FINANCIAL INSTITUTION

Context

A large financial institution is undertaking a significant IT system upgrade to enhance its digital banking services. The project involves complex technical elements and requires careful risk management, particularly in terms of stakeholder engagement.

Collaborating with the Team

- **Formation of a Risk Management Team:** Comprising IT specialists, project managers, and representatives from key departments like finance, operations, and customer service.

- **Regular Meetings:** Scheduling regular meetings to discuss risk planning, assessment, and response strategies.

Leveraging Stakeholder Analysis

- **Utilizing Project Manager's Analysis:** Building on the stakeholder analysis conducted by the project manager to understand the interests, influence, and expectations of various stakeholders.

- **Identifying Stakeholder Concerns:** Paying special attention to stakeholders' concerns regarding system downtime, data security, and customer experience.

Managing Stakeholder Risk Appetite and Attitudes

- **Risk Appetite Assessment:** Gauging the risk tolerance of different stakeholder groups, especially in areas like system security and operational continuity.

- **Addressing Concerns:** Developing strategies to align stakeholder attitudes with the project's risk management approach.

Engaging Stakeholders in Risk Prioritization

- **Inclusive Workshops:** Organizing workshops where stakeholders can contribute to the risk prioritization process.

- **Transparent Criteria:** Ensuring the criteria for prioritizing risks are clear and understood by all stakeholders.

Setting Expectations for Engagement

- **Communication of Rules:** Clearly communicating the rules of engagement in risk management, such as responsibilities, reporting structures, and decision-making processes.

- **Expectation Management:** Setting realistic expectations regarding risk management outcomes and timelines.

Tailoring Risk Communication

- **Customized Messages:** Tailoring communication to suit the specific needs and understanding levels of different stakeholder groups.

- **Regular Updates:** Providing consistent and timely updates about risk status and management activities.

Leading Stakeholder Empowerment

- **Involvement in Strategy Development:** Encouraging stakeholders to actively participate in developing and refining the risk management strategies.

- **Ownership of Risk Areas:** Allowing stakeholders to take ownership of certain risk areas relevant to their expertise or interest.

Training, Coaching, and Educating Stakeholders

- **Training Sessions:** Organizing regular training sessions on risk management principles and processes.

- **Coaching for Key Personnel:** Providing one-on-one coaching to key stakeholders to deepen their understanding of risk management.

- **Educational Materials:** Distributing easy-to-understand guides and FAQs on risk management principles and processes.

Conclusion

In the context of the IT system upgrade project in the financial institution, planning and leading risk management activities with stakeholders involve a collaborative approach. By leveraging existing stakeholder analysis, managing risk appetite, engaging stakeholders in prioritization, setting clear rules of engagement, tailoring communication, empowering stakeholders, and providing training and education, the project risk manager ensures a comprehensive and inclusive risk management process. This approach not only aligns with PMI standards but also fosters stakeholder engagement and ownership in the risk management process, crucial for the successful and secure upgrade of the IT systems.

DOMAIN II
RISK
IDENTIFICATION

Task 1 Conduct risk identification exercises

COORDINATION OF MEETINGS, INTERVIEWS, FOCUS GROUPS, AND SME SUPPORT ACTIVITIES

Conducting meetings, interviews, focus groups, and other Subject Matter Expert (SME) support activities is an integral part of Domain II Risk Identification, Task 1 in risk management. These activities are crucial for gathering diverse insights and identifying potential risks in a project. Here's how to effectively conduct these activities:

1. Conducting Meetings

- **Purpose**: To bring together project team members and stakeholders to discuss and identify potential risks.

- **Preparation**: Prepare an agenda that outlines the key topics for risk discussion. Include time for open discussion to uncover risks that may not be immediately apparent.

- **Participant Selection**: Include individuals with various project roles and perspectives to ensure a comprehensive view of potential risks.

- **Facilitation**: Facilitate the meeting to encourage participation from all attendees, ensuring that different viewpoints are heard and considered.

2. Conducting Interviews

- **Purpose**: To gather in-depth insights from individuals, particularly those with specific expertise or experience relevant to the project.

- **Targeted Interviews**: Identify and interview key personnel, including project sponsors, team leaders, and external stakeholders, to gain detailed understanding of potential risks.

- **Structured Approach**: Use a structured set of questions to guide the interview while allowing for open-ended responses that can reveal unexpected risks.

3. Organizing Focus Groups

- **Purpose**: To facilitate a structured discussion among a group of participants to identify risks through collective insights.

- **Diverse Groups**: Assemble groups with diverse backgrounds and knowledge areas relevant to the project.

- **Moderation**: Moderate the discussions to encourage interaction and brainstorming, and to prevent dominance by any single participant.

4. Engaging Subject Matter Experts (SMEs)

- **Purpose**: To leverage specialized knowledge and experience that SMEs possess in identifying and analyzing risks.

- **Expert Selection**: Choose experts based on their specific knowledge areas that are relevant to the project's scope and objectives.

- **Consultation Methods**: Engage SMEs through one-on-one consultations, expert panels, or workshops.

5. Documenting the Process

- **Record Keeping**: Keep detailed records of all meetings, interviews, focus groups, and SME consultations. This includes minutes, interview notes, and summaries of discussions.

- **Identifying Risk Themes**: Look for common themes or recurring concerns that emerge from these activities, as they may indicate significant risks.

6. Analyzing and Synthesizing Information

- **Review and Analysis**: After conducting these activities, review and analyze the collected information to identify potential risks.

- **Synthesis**: Synthesize insights from different sources to form a comprehensive understanding of the risks facing the project.

Conclusion

Meetings, interviews, focus groups, and SME consultations are essential methods for thorough risk identification. They provide a platform for stakeholders to share their knowledge and perspectives, contributing to a more complete and nuanced understanding of potential project risks. Effective planning, facilitation, and documentation of these activities are key to ensuring their success.

IN-DEPTH ANALYSIS OF RISK IDENTIFICATION EXERCISE OUTCOMES

Performing detailed analyses of risk identification exercise results is a crucial step in Domain II Risk Identification, Task 1. This process involves examining the information gathered from various risk identification activities such as meetings, interviews, and focus groups to identify potential risks. Here's a structured approach to conducting this analysis:

1. Compiling and Organizing Data

- **Gather All Information**: Compile all data collected from risk identification exercises, including meeting notes, interview transcripts, focus group summaries, and feedback from SMEs.

- **Organization**: Organize the information in a structured format, such as a spreadsheet or a database, for easy analysis.

2. Identifying Potential Risks

- **Extraction of Risks**: Go through the compiled data to extract potential risks. Look for direct mentions of risks, concerns raised by stakeholders, or issues that were discussed repeatedly.

- **Categorization**: Categorize the identified risks into relevant groups (e.g., technical, financial, operational, environmental).

3. Analyzing for Common Themes and Trends

- **Theme Identification**: Identify common themes or trends that emerge from the data. This could indicate areas with higher risk concentrations.

- **Cross-Referencing**: Cross-reference the findings with project documents and historical data to validate and add context to the identified risks.

4. Prioritizing Risks

- **Risk Ranking**: Rank the identified risks based on factors like their potential impact, likelihood of occurrence, and the urgency of addressing them.

- **Use of Risk Matrix**: Employ a risk matrix to help visualize and prioritize risks according to their severity.

5. Validating Risks with Stakeholders

- **Stakeholder Validation**: Present the identified risks back to key stakeholders to validate your findings and gather additional insights.

- **Refinement**: Refine the list of risks based on stakeholder feedback and additional analysis.

6. Documenting Risk Attributes

- **Detailed Documentation**: For each identified risk, document its attributes including descriptions, causes, potential impacts, and affected areas of the project.

- **Risk Ownership**: Assign an owner to each risk, who will be responsible for monitoring and managing that risk.

7. Developing an Initial Response Plan

- **Response Strategies**: For high-priority risks, start developing initial risk response strategies.

- **Inclusion in Risk Register**: Include these risks and their initial response strategies in the risk register.

8. Continuous Monitoring and Updating

- **Regular Reviews**: Regularly review the identified risks to ensure they are still relevant and to identify any new risks.

- **Dynamic Updating**: Update the risk analysis as the project progresses and as more information becomes available.

Conclusion

The detailed analysis of risk identification exercise results is a systematic process that involves organizing, extracting, analyzing, and validating the identified risks. It requires close examination of collected data, prioritization of risks, and continuous engagement with stakeholders. This thorough analysis is critical for developing an effective risk management plan that is responsive to the specific needs and challenges of the project.

COMPREHENSIVE ANALYSIS OF VARIOUS INFORMATION SOURCES WITHIN BUSINESS CONTEXT

Analyzing documents, audio transcripts, telemetry data, and other forms of information is an essential part of risk identification in project management. This analysis not only involves a technical examination of the data but also an understanding of the business context in which this information exists. Here's a guide to performing this analysis effectively:

1. Gathering and Organizing Information

- **Collect Data**: Assemble all relevant documents, audio transcripts, telemetry data, and other pertinent information.

- **Organization**: Organize this data in a systematic way for ease of analysis. This could involve creating a database or using project management software.

2. Technical Analysis

- **Document Review**: Thoroughly review documents for any indications of potential risks. This includes project plans, reports, contractual documents, and correspondence.

- **Audio Transcripts**: Listen to and analyze audio recordings of meetings, interviews, or discussions, focusing on mentions of challenges, concerns, or uncertainties.

- **Telemetry Data Analysis**: For telemetry data (which could include a range of technical data points), use appropriate tools and software to analyze patterns, anomalies, or trends that could signify risks.

3. Understanding Business Context

- **Project Objectives and Environment**: Understand the project's objectives and the business environment in which it operates. This includes market conditions, organizational culture, and strategic goals.

- **Stakeholder Perspectives**: Consider the perspectives and interests of different stakeholders. Understanding their views can provide insights into potential risks.

4. Identifying Risk Indicators

- **Signs of Risks**: Look for indicators of risks in the information. This could be subtle hints in conversation transcripts, trends in telemetry data, or discrepancies in documents.

- **Cross-Referencing**: Cross-reference these indicators with other project information to validate potential risks.

5. Consulting Subject Matter Experts (SMEs)

- **Expert Insights**: Consult SMEs to gain deeper insights into technical data or to understand complex information.

- **Validation of Findings**: Use their expertise to validate or refute potential risks identified during the analysis.

6. Documenting Findings

- **Risk Documentation**: Document the findings from the analysis, focusing on how each piece of information relates to potential project risks.

- **Contextual Analysis**: Include an explanation of how the business context influences these risks.

7. Stakeholder Communication

- **Sharing Findings**: Communicate the findings of the analysis with relevant stakeholders.

- **Feedback Loop**: Encourage stakeholders to provide feedback or additional insights to further refine the risk analysis.

8. Continuous Monitoring and Updating

- **Ongoing Analysis**: Continuously monitor and analyze new documents, transcripts, and data as they become available.

- **Adaptation**: Be prepared to adapt the risk analysis based on new information and changing project dynamics.

Conclusion

Analyzing various forms of data for risk identification is a multifaceted process that requires technical scrutiny and a deep understanding of the business context. It involves careful examination of documents, audio transcripts, and telemetry data, supplemented by SME consultations and stakeholder feedback. This thorough analysis is crucial for identifying potential risks early in the project lifecycle and developing appropriate risk management strategies.

CATEGORIZATION OF RISKS AS THREATS OR OPPORTUNITIES

Indicating risks as threats or opportunities is a key aspect of risk identification and analysis in project management. This approach recognizes that risks not only present potential negative impacts (threats) but can also offer positive possibilities (opportunities). Properly categorizing risks as either threats or opportunities allows for more effective risk response planning. Here's how to approach this task:

1. Understanding the Nature of Risks

- **Definition of Threats**: Threats are potential risks that could negatively impact the project, such as delays, cost overruns, or quality issues.

- **Definition of Opportunities**: Opportunities are potential risks that could have a positive impact on the project, leading to benefits like cost savings, time efficiencies, or enhanced quality.

2. Analyzing Risk Characteristics

- **Review Risk Data**: Examine each identified risk, considering factors like its source, nature, and potential impact on the project.

- **Assess Impact and Likelihood**: Evaluate both the likelihood of occurrence and the potential impact (negative or positive) of each risk.

3. Categorizing Risks

- **Categorize as Threat or Opportunity**: Based on the analysis, categorize each risk as a threat or an opportunity.

- **Use of Risk Matrix**: Employ a risk matrix to visually map out risks, helping in the categorization process.

4. Consulting with Stakeholders

- **Stakeholder Perspectives**: Engage stakeholders in the categorization process to leverage their insights and perspectives.

- **Validation**: Use stakeholder feedback to validate the categorization of risks as threats or opportunities.

5. Documenting Risk Categories

- **Risk Register**: Record the categorized risks in the risk register, clearly indicating whether each risk is a threat or an opportunity.

- **Detailed Descriptions**: Provide detailed descriptions of why each risk is categorized as a threat or an opportunity.

6. Planning for Risk Responses

- **Response Strategies for Threats**: Develop response strategies for threats, such as avoidance, mitigation, transfer, or acceptance.

- **Exploiting Opportunities**: Plan how to exploit or enhance opportunities, potentially using strategies like exploiting, sharing, enhancing, or accepting.

7. Regular Review and Reassessment

- **Ongoing Assessment**: Regularly review and reassess risks to ensure they are correctly categorized, as new information might change their nature.

- **Adaptability**: Be prepared to adapt risk response strategies if a risk's categorization changes over the course of the project.

Conclusion

Accurately indicating risks as threats or opportunities is an essential part of effective risk management. This process involves careful analysis, stakeholder consultation, and thorough documentation. By distinguishing between threats and opportunities, project teams can develop more targeted and effective strategies for managing risks, thereby enhancing the potential for project success.

CASE STUDY: NEW PRODUCT LAUNCH IN A CONSUMER ELECTRONICS COMPANY

Context

A leading consumer electronics company is preparing to launch a new line of smart home devices. To ensure the success of this launch, conducting thorough risk identification exercises is critical. The project risk manager oversees this process, focusing on identifying both potential threats and opportunities.

Conducting Meetings, Interviews, and Focus Groups

- **Team Meetings:** Organizing regular meetings with the project team to brainstorm and identify potential risks.

- **Expert Interviews:** Conducting interviews with subject matter experts (SMEs) in areas like product development, market trends, and consumer behavior.

- **Focus Groups:** Holding focus groups with potential consumers to gather insights on user preferences, usability concerns, and market acceptance.

SME Support Activities

- **Consultation with Technical Experts:** Engaging with engineers and IT specialists to identify technical risks related to product design and functionality.

- **Market Analysis:** Collaborating with marketing experts to understand market trends and competitive landscape.

Performing Detailed Analyses of Risk Identification Exercise Results

- **Data Synthesis:** Compiling and analyzing data from meetings, interviews, and focus groups to identify recurring themes and unique risks.

- **Risk Categorization:** Classifying identified risks into categories such as market risks, technical risks, supply chain risks, etc.

Analyzing Documents, Transcripts, and Telemetry Data

- **Document Review:** Examining project documents, market reports, and previous product launch reviews for potential risk indicators.

- **Audio Transcript Analysis:** Analyzing transcripts from interviews and focus groups for nuanced insights.

Alexander Stratton

- **Telemetry Data Analysis:** Reviewing data from product prototypes and testing phases to identify technical and usability risks.

Understanding Business Context of Information

- **Market Positioning:** Considering how the new product fits into the company's overall market strategy.

- **Brand Reputation:** Assessing risks in the context of the company's brand reputation and customer loyalty.

Indicating Risks as Threats or Opportunities

- **Threat Identification:** Recognizing risks that could negatively impact the product launch, such as supply chain disruptions, technical failures, or negative market reception.

- **Opportunity Recognition:** Identifying potential opportunities that could arise, such as tapping into a new customer segment or leveraging advanced technology for a competitive edge.

Conclusion

In this case, conducting risk identification exercises for the new product launch involves a multifaceted approach that includes meetings, interviews, focus groups, and detailed analyses of various data sources. By analyzing documents, audio transcripts, and telemetry data, the project risk manager is able to understand the business context and differentiate between risks that present threats and those that offer opportunities. This comprehensive approach ensures that the risk management process is thorough and aligned with the company's strategic objectives, thereby enhancing the likelihood of a successful product launch in the competitive consumer electronics market.

Task 2 Examine assumption and constraint analyses

UTILIZATION OF ASSUMPTION AND CONSTRAINT ANALYSIS OUTCOMES

Leveraging the results of the assumption and constraint analysis is a critical task in risk management, particularly in the examination of assumptions and constraints for a project. This process involves utilizing the insights gained from analyzing project assumptions and constraints to inform and enhance the risk management strategy. Here's how to effectively leverage these results:

1. Review and Understand Assumptions and Constraints

- **Assumptions Analysis**: Review the identified assumptions which are the 'givens' considered true for the project's planning and execution. These might include expectations about resources, timelines, technology, and stakeholder support.

- **Constraints Analysis**: Understand the constraints that are limitations or restrictions impacting the project, such as budgetary limits, resource availability, regulatory requirements, and fixed deadlines.

2. Integrate into Risk Identification

- **Identify Risks Linked to Assumptions**: Recognize that assumptions could be incorrect or might change, leading to potential risks. For instance, an assumption about the availability of a critical resource might lead to risks if that resource becomes unavailable.

- **Identify Risks from Constraints**: Constraints often breed risks. For example, budget constraints could lead to risks around cutting corners or not having sufficient funds to cover unexpected costs.

3. Evaluate Impact on Project Objectives

- **Impact Analysis**: Assess how these assumptions and constraints might impact the achievement of project objectives. Determine whether they could lead to scope, schedule, quality, or cost issues.

- **Scenario Planning**: Use scenario planning to understand the potential impacts if an assumption proves false or a constraint becomes more restrictive.

4. Incorporate into Risk Analysis and Prioritization

- **Risk Prioritization**: Prioritize risks arising from assumptions and constraints based on their likelihood and potential impact on project objectives.

- **Quantitative and Qualitative Analysis**: Use both qualitative and quantitative methods to analyze these risks.

5. Develop Response Strategies

- **Plan for Assumption Changes**: Develop contingency plans in case key assumptions change. This might include alternative strategies or additional resources.

- **Mitigate Constraint Risks**: Identify ways to mitigate risks arising from constraints, such as seeking additional funding or optimizing resource allocation.

6. Communication and Stakeholder Engagement

- **Communicate with Stakeholders**: Clearly communicate the identified risks related to assumptions and constraints to relevant stakeholders.

- **Stakeholder Input**: Encourage stakeholders to provide their insights and to challenge assumptions and constraints, leading to a more robust risk analysis.

7. Regular Review and Update

- **Monitor Assumptions and Constraints**: Regularly review the assumptions and constraints throughout the project lifecycle as they may change over time, necessitating adjustments in the risk management plan.

Conclusion

Leveraging the results of assumption and constraint analysis is essential in identifying potential risks and developing effective risk management strategies. It requires a thorough understanding of how these assumptions and constraints might affect project objectives and involves continuous monitoring, stakeholder engagement, and proactive planning to mitigate potential risks. This approach ensures that risks are not only identified but also managed proactively, enhancing the project's likelihood of success.

CATEGORIZATION OF PROJECT ASSUMPTIONS AND CONSTRAINTS

Categorizing assumptions and constraints in project risk management involves organizing them into meaningful groups or categories. This categorization helps in understanding their nature, potential impact on the project, and how they should be managed. Here's a structured approach to categorizing assumptions and constraints:

1. Understanding Assumptions and Constraints

- **Assumptions**: Assumptions are beliefs or statements taken to be true without proof at the beginning of the project. They are based on previous experiences or accepted practices.

- **Constraints**: Constraints are limitations or restrictions that affect the project's execution, such as time, budget, resources, and technology.

2. Categories of Assumptions

- **Resource Assumptions**: Availability, productivity, and capability of resources (human, material, equipment).

- **Technical Assumptions**: Assumptions related to technology, technical processes, or systems.

- **Stakeholder Assumptions**: Expectations about stakeholder involvement, support, and influence.

- **Environmental Assumptions**: Assumptions regarding the project's external environment, such as market conditions or regulatory landscape.

- **Schedule Assumptions**: Assumptions about timelines, project milestones, and deadlines.

3. Categories of Constraints

- **Budgetary Constraints**: Limits related to the project's finances, such as budget caps or funding availability.

- **Time Constraints**: Deadlines, fixed dates, or schedule limitations impacting the project.

- **Resource Constraints**: Availability or limitations of resources, including workforce, equipment, and materials.

- **Scope Constraints**: Boundaries of what the project can or cannot deliver.

- **Regulatory and Compliance Constraints**: Legal or regulatory requirements that the project must adhere to.

4. Categorization Process

- **Review Project Documentation**: Go through project documents to identify stated or implied assumptions and constraints.

- **Engage with Stakeholders**: Discuss with project stakeholders to uncover any additional assumptions and constraints.

- **Grouping**: Group similar assumptions and constraints together into the identified categories.

5. Documenting Assumptions and Constraints

- **Risk Register or Project Plan**: Document the categorized assumptions and constraints in the project plan or risk register.

- **Clarity and Accessibility**: Ensure that the documentation is clear and easily accessible to relevant stakeholders.

6. Regular Review and Adjustment

- **Periodic Reviews**: Regularly review and update the categories of assumptions and constraints to reflect any changes in the project environment or scope.

- **Adaptation**: Be prepared to adapt the project plan and risk management strategies based on changes in assumptions and constraints.

Conclusion

Categorizing assumptions and constraints is a crucial step in risk management that helps in their effective analysis and monitoring. It provides clarity on potential risk areas and supports the development of targeted risk responses. Regular review and communication with stakeholders about these assumptions and constraints are essential for keeping the risk management process relevant and dynamic.

ASSESSMENT OF RISK ASSOCIATED WITH PROJECT ASSUMPTIONS AND CONSTRAINTS

Assessing the risk associated with each assumption and/or constraint is an essential task in risk management, as it helps in identifying potential areas where the project might face challenges. This assessment involves evaluating how likely each assumption is to be false or how each constraint might impact the project negatively. Here's a structured approach to this assessment:

1. Review and List Assumptions and Constraints

- **Documentation Review**: Begin by reviewing project documentation to list all identified assumptions and constraints.

- **Stakeholder Input**: Consult with stakeholders to ensure that all relevant assumptions and constraints have been captured.

2. Evaluate the Validity of Assumptions

- **Likelihood of Change**: Assess how likely it is that an assumption may prove to be incorrect. Consider historical data, expert opinions, and current project context.

- **Impact of Invalid Assumptions**: Determine the potential impact on the project if an assumption is found to be false. How would it affect the project's scope, schedule, budget, or quality?

3. Analyze the Impact of Constraints

- **Constraint Limitations**: Evaluate how each constraint limits the project. For example, budget constraints might limit the quality of materials used.

- **Consequence Analysis**: Analyze the consequences of each constraint on the project's objectives. For instance, how would time constraints affect project deliverables?

4. Risk Rating for Assumptions and Constraints

- **Prioritization**: Based on the likelihood and impact assessments, prioritize the risks associated with each assumption and constraint.

- **Risk Matrix Use**: Utilize a risk matrix to visually map out and rate these risks, aiding in prioritization and communication.

5. Develop Contingency and Mitigation Plans

- **Contingency Planning**: For assumptions with high-risk ratings, develop contingency plans to address the risks should the assumptions prove false.

- **Mitigation Strategies**: For constraints that pose significant risks, identify mitigation strategies to minimize their impact.

6. Stakeholder Communication

- **Inform Stakeholders**: Communicate the findings of the risk assessment to stakeholders, especially those risks that are high priority.

- **Feedback Integration**: Integrate feedback from stakeholders to refine the risk assessment.

7. Documenting the Assessment

- **Risk Register**: Document the risk assessment of each assumption and constraint in the risk register.

- **Detailed Descriptions**: Provide detailed descriptions of the risk assessment process, findings, and any planned responses.

8. Regular Monitoring and Review

- **Continuous Monitoring**: Regularly monitor the assumptions and constraints throughout the project lifecycle for any changes.

- **Review and Update**: Periodically review and update the risk assessment to reflect any new information or changes in the project environment.

Conclusion

Assessing the risk associated with each assumption and constraint allows for a proactive approach to risk management. It helps in identifying potential problem areas early and enables the development of effective strategies to address these risks. Regular review and stakeholder engagement are key to ensuring that this assessment remains accurate and relevant throughout the project.

UNDERSTANDING THE INTERPLAY BETWEEN ASSUMPTIONS/CONSTRAINTS AND PROJECT OBJECTIVES

Recognizing the relationship between assumptions and/or constraints and project objectives is a vital aspect of risk management. This process involves understanding how assumptions and constraints can directly or indirectly impact the achievement of project goals. By examining these relationships, you can anticipate potential issues and plan accordingly. Here's how to approach this analysis:

1. Map Assumptions and Constraints to Project Objectives

- **Alignment Analysis**: Review each project objective and align it with relevant assumptions and constraints. For example, if one objective is to complete the project within a specific timeframe, align this with assumptions about resource availability and constraints like fixed deadlines.

- **Impact Assessment**: Assess how each assumption or constraint could impact the achievement of the corresponding objective.

2. Analyze the Potential Impact

- **Positive and Negative Effects**: Consider both the positive and negative impacts of assumptions and constraints on project objectives. For instance, a constraint like a fixed budget can negatively impact the scope, while an assumption of continuous stakeholder support can positively influence project success.

- **Cascading Effects**: Understand the cascading effects where one assumption or constraint impacts multiple objectives or triggers other risks. For example, stakeholders' holiday schedules might delay key decisions, affecting the project timeline and potentially increasing costs due to delays.

3. Scenario Planning

- **Best and Worst-case Scenarios**: Develop scenarios based on assumptions being true or false and constraints being stringent or relaxed. Analyze how these scenarios could affect project objectives.

- **Sensitivity Analysis**: Conduct sensitivity analysis to determine which assumptions and constraints are most critical to project success.

4. Stakeholder Consultation

- **Engage Stakeholders**: Discuss with stakeholders to gain their perspectives on the potential impact of assumptions and constraints on project objectives.

- **Feedback Incorporation**: Use stakeholder feedback to refine the understanding of these relationships.

5. Documenting the Analysis

- **Detailed Documentation**: Document the findings of the analysis, highlighting how specific assumptions and constraints relate to and impact project objectives.

- **Risk Register Updates**: Update the risk register to include risks arising from the relationship between assumptions, constraints, and objectives.

6. Develop Contingency and Response Plans

- **Prepare for Impact**: Based on the analysis, develop contingency and response plans for scenarios where assumptions prove false or constraints become more restrictive.

- **Mitigation Strategies**: Create mitigation strategies for risks that could significantly derail project objectives.

7. Regular Review and Adjustment

- **Dynamic Review Process**: Regularly review and adjust the analysis as the project progresses and new information comes to light.

- **Adaptability**: Be prepared to adapt project plans and strategies in response to changes in assumptions and constraints.

Conclusion

Recognizing the relationship between assumptions, constraints, and project objectives is key to anticipating potential impacts on project success. This understanding allows for proactive planning and effective risk management, ensuring that project objectives are met despite uncertainties. Regular reviews and stakeholder engagement are crucial in keeping this analysis relevant and actionable throughout the project lifecycle.

PROMOTION OF STAKEHOLDER ENGAGEMENT IN CHALLENGING ASSUMPTIONS AND CONSTRAINTS

Encouraging stakeholders to challenge assumptions and constraints is a vital part of risk management. This approach promotes critical thinking and helps uncover potential risks that might not be immediately apparent. It involves creating an environment where questioning and reassessing established beliefs and limitations are not only accepted but encouraged. Here's how to approach this:

1. Foster an Open Communication Culture

- **Promote Openness**: Create an environment where stakeholders feel comfortable expressing their opinions and challenging the status quo.

- **Regular Forums**: Hold regular meetings or forums where stakeholders can discuss and question project assumptions and constraints.

2. Educate Stakeholders on the Importance of Challenging Assumptions

- **Awareness Sessions**: Conduct sessions to educate stakeholders about the importance of critically assessing assumptions and constraints.

- **Showcase Examples**: Use past project examples where unchallenged assumptions or constraints led to issues, demonstrating the value of scrutiny.

3. Actively Solicit Feedback and Opinions

- **Surveys and Questionnaires**: Use tools like surveys or questionnaires to gather stakeholders' views on various project assumptions and constraints.

- **Direct Engagement**: Engage directly with stakeholders, asking for their input and encouraging them to voice any concerns or alternate views.

4. Encourage Diverse Perspectives

- **Diversity of Thought**: Ensure that the project team and stakeholder group include individuals with diverse backgrounds and perspectives.

- **Cross-Functional Workshops**: Organize workshops with participants from different areas of expertise to look at assumptions and constraints from various angles.

5. Reward Constructive Challenge

- **Recognition**: Acknowledge and reward stakeholders who constructively challenge assumptions and contribute to uncovering potential risks.

- **Positive Reinforcement**: Publicly praise critical thinking and constructive challenges to encourage others to follow suit.

6. Utilize Critical Thinking Techniques

- **Brainstorming Sessions**: Conduct brainstorming sessions focused on questioning and reevaluating project assumptions and constraints.

- **'What If' Scenarios**: Use 'what if' scenarios to explore the implications of assumptions being incorrect or constraints changing.

7. Review and Reassess Assumptions and Constraints Regularly

- **Scheduled Reviews**: Set up regular intervals for reviewing and reassessing assumptions and constraints.

- **Dynamic Adjustment**: Be open to adjusting project plans and strategies based on the outcomes of these reviews.

8. Lead by Example

- **Model Behavior**: Project leaders should model the behavior by regularly questioning and reassessing their own assumptions and constraints.

- **Transparency in Decision-Making**: Show how stakeholder input, especially challenges to assumptions, is incorporated into decision making.

Conclusion

Encouraging stakeholders to challenge assumptions and constraints is essential for a robust and proactive risk management process. It helps in uncovering hidden risks and ensures that the project plan is resilient and adaptable. This approach requires a culture of open communication, ongoing education, and recognition of the value of diverse perspectives and critical thinking.

CASE STUDY: INTERNATIONAL EXPANSION OF A RETAIL CHAIN

Context

A global retail chain is planning an international expansion into new markets. The project involves significant assumptions and constraints that could impact its success. The project risk manager is responsible for examining these assumptions and constraints and assessing their associated risks.

Leveraging Assumption and Constraint Analysis Results

- **Initial Analysis:** Reviewing the initial assumption and constraint analysis conducted during the project planning phase.

- **Key Findings:** Identifying critical assumptions made about market demand, supply chain logistics, and local regulatory environments.

Categorizing Assumptions and Constraints

- **Market-Related Assumptions:** Consumer behavior, market demand, and competition.

- **Operational Constraints:** Supply chain limitations, staffing challenges, and store setup times.

- **Regulatory Constraints:** Local laws, trade regulations, and compliance requirements.

Assessing Risks Associated with Assumptions and Constraints

- **Risk Evaluation:** Assessing the likelihood and impact of each assumption or constraint not holding true.

- **Sensitivity Analysis:** Analyzing how sensitive the project's success is to changes in key assumptions and constraints.

Recognizing Relationships Between Assumptions/Constraints and Project Objectives

- **Impact Analysis:** Understanding how assumptions and constraints directly affect project objectives, such as market penetration, revenue targets, and timelines.

- **Cascade Effect Example:** Predicting how stakeholders' holiday schedules might delay key decisions and thus affect project timelines. For example, delays in regulatory approvals due to holiday schedules could push back store openings, impacting revenue projections.

Encouraging Stakeholders to Challenge Assumptions and Constraints

- **Open Forums:** Creating opportunities for stakeholders to discuss and challenge assumptions and constraints, such as through workshops or meetings.

- **Critical Thinking:** Promoting a culture of critical thinking where questioning assumptions is encouraged and valued.

- **Scenario Planning:** Using scenario planning exercises to explore what could happen if key assumptions are incorrect or constraints are tighter or looser than expected.

Conclusion

In the context of the international expansion project of the retail chain, examining assumption and constraint analyses is a critical step in risk management. By categorizing, assessing, and understanding the relationships between assumptions, constraints, and project objectives, the project risk manager can better predict potential risks and their impacts. Encouraging stakeholders to actively challenge assumptions and constraints ensures a more robust and resilient planning process. This approach aligns with PMI standards for risk management and is essential for the successful international expansion of the retail chain, helping to navigate the complexities of new market entries.

Task 3 Document risk triggers and thresholds based on context/environment

EVALUATION AND DOCUMENTATION OF RISK COMPLIANCE THRESHOLDS AND CATEGORIES AGAINST UPDATED RISK DATA

Assessing, confirming, and documenting risk compliance thresholds and categories against updated risk data is an essential task in the risk management process. This task involves determining the acceptable levels of risk for the project and ensuring they align with the latest information and data. Here's how to approach this:

1. Assessing Compliance Thresholds

- **Understand Compliance Requirements**: Review and understand the regulatory, legal, and organizational compliance requirements relevant to the project.

- **Determine Thresholds**: Based on these requirements, determine the thresholds for acceptable risk levels. For instance, this could involve setting limits on cost overruns, schedule delays, or quality standards.

2. Gathering and Updating Risk Data

- **Collect Updated Data**: Gather the most recent data on identified risks, including changes in risk probability, impact, and any new risks that have emerged.

- **Data Sources**: Use a variety of sources for risk data, including project reports, stakeholder feedback, and industry benchmarks.

3. Reviewing and Adjusting Thresholds

- **Comparison with New Data**: Compare the existing compliance thresholds with the updated risk data to see if they still align.

- **Adjust Thresholds as Needed**: Adjust the compliance thresholds if the new data indicates changes in the risk landscape, such as new regulatory requirements or altered project conditions.

4. Categorizing Risks

- **Categories Based on Compliance**: Categorize risks based on compliance related aspects, such as legal risks, environmental risks, financial compliance risks, etc.

- **Prioritization Within Categories**: Prioritize risks within each category based on their potential impact on compliance.

5. Documenting Thresholds and Categories

- **Clear Documentation**: Document the compliance thresholds and risk categories in a clear and accessible format.

- **Inclusion in Risk Register**: Incorporate this information into the project's risk register or a separate compliance document.

6. Stakeholder Consultation and Confirmation

- **Engage Stakeholders**: Consult with stakeholders, including project team members, legal advisors, and compliance officers, to confirm the appropriateness of the thresholds and categories.

- **Feedback Integration**: Integrate feedback to refine the compliance thresholds and risk categorization.

7. Regular Review and Updates

- **Dynamic Process**: Treat the assessment of compliance thresholds as a dynamic process, requiring regular reviews and updates as project conditions and external factors change.

Conclusion

Assessing, confirming, and documenting risk compliance thresholds against updated risk data is crucial for ensuring that the project remains within acceptable risk parameters. This process involves understanding compliance requirements, regularly updating and analyzing risk data, adjusting thresholds as necessary, and categorizing risks accordingly. Effective documentation and regular stakeholder engagement are key to maintaining accurate and relevant compliance thresholds throughout the project lifecycle.

ASSESSMENT AND DOCUMENTATION OF RISK TRIGGERS, CAUSES, AND TIMING

Assessing and documenting risk triggers, causes, and timing is a crucial component of effective risk management. This process involves identifying the specific conditions or events that could initiate a risk, understanding the underlying causes of these risks, and determining when they are likely to occur. Here's how to approach this task:

1. Identifying Risk Triggers

- **Definition of Triggers**: Risk triggers are specific events or conditions that indicate the onset of a risk.

- **Identification**: Review each identified risk and determine what could potentially trigger it. For example, a trigger for a budget risk could be the receipt of an unexpectedly high supplier invoice.

2. Understanding Risk Causes

- **Root Cause Analysis**: For each risk, perform a root cause analysis to understand why the risk may occur.

- **Factors Contributing to Risk**: Identify internal and external factors that contribute to the risk These could include project complexity, external market conditions, or resource constraints.

3. Determining Timing of Risks

- **Assess Timing**: Evaluate when each risk is most likely to occur within the project lifecycle. This can be based on project milestones, external events, or other timelines.

- **Probability Over Time**: Understand that the probability of a risk occurring might change over time, increasing or decreasing as the project progresses.

4. Documenting Triggers, Causes, and Timing

- **Risk Register Entries**: Document the identified triggers, causes, and timing for each risk in the risk register.

- **Clear Descriptions**: Provide clear and detailed descriptions to ensure that the information is easily understood and actionable.

5. Developing Monitoring Strategies

- **Trigger-Based Monitoring**: Set up monitoring strategies for identified triggers to catch risks early. For example, monitoring market trends for risks related to material cost increases.

- **Alert Systems**: Consider establishing alert systems for critical triggers to notify the relevant stakeholders immediately.

6. Stakeholder Communication

- **Informing Stakeholders**: Communicate the identified triggers, causes, and timing to all relevant stakeholders, ensuring they are aware of what to watch for.

- **Feedback Loop**: Encourage stakeholders to provide feedback or additional information that could refine the risk assessment.

7. Regular Review and Updates

- **Dynamic Assessment**: Regularly review and update the assessment of triggers, causes, and timing to reflect new information or changes in the project environment.

- **Adjustments in Plan**: Be prepared to adjust risk management plans and strategies in response to changes in risk triggers and causes.

Conclusion

Assessing and documenting risk triggers, causes, and timing is essential for proactive risk management. It enables the project team to monitor for specific indicators of risk, understand the underlying factors contributing to risk, and anticipate when risks are most likely to occur. This detailed documentation, combined with regular reviews and stakeholder communication, ensures that the project team is well-prepared to manage risks effectively.

ASSESSMENT AND DOCUMENTATION OF RISK CONSEQUENCES AND IMPACT

Assessing and documenting risk consequences and/or impact is a critical step in risk management. It involves evaluating the potential effects of risks on a project's objectives, such as scope, schedule, budget, and quality. Proper documentation of these assessments aids in prioritizing risks and developing effective mitigation strategies. Here's a structured approach to this task:

1. Evaluating Risk Consequences

- **Quantitative and Qualitative Assessment**: Assess the potential impact of each risk both quantitatively (e.g., cost or time overruns) and qualitatively (e.g., reputational damage, safety concerns).

- **Scope of Impact**: Determine how each risk could affect different aspects of the project, such as delays in milestones, increased costs, or degradation of quality.

2. Understanding Direct and Indirect Impact

- **Direct Impact**: Evaluate the immediate effects of the risk event materializing. For example, the direct impact of a critical resource becoming unavailable.

- **Indirect Impact**: Consider secondary effects or cascading impacts. For instance, a delay in one task might lead to subsequent delays in other dependent tasks.

3. Prioritizing Risks Based on Impact

- **Risk Rating**: Prioritize risks based on the severity of their consequences. High-impact risks require more immediate attention and robust response strategies.

- **Risk Matrix**: Use a risk matrix to categorize risks according to their impact and likelihood, aiding in prioritization.

4. Documenting Risk Impact

- **Risk Register Entries**: Document the assessed impact of each risk in the risk register or a dedicated risk impact analysis document.

- **Detailing Consequences**: Provide detailed descriptions of potential consequences, including possible financial, operational, and strategic impacts.

5. Consulting with Stakeholders

- **Stakeholder Insights**: Engage with stakeholders to get their perspective on the potential impact of risks. They may provide additional insights or highlight impacts you hadn't considered.

- **Validation of Impact Assessment**: Use stakeholder feedback to validate or adjust your impact assessments.

6. Linking to Project Objectives

- **Alignment with Objectives**: Relate the potential impact of risks to specific project objectives. Understanding this relationship helps in aligning risk management efforts with project goals.

- **Objective-Based Prioritization**: Prioritize risks based on their potential to derail critical project objectives.

7. Review and Update Impact Assessments

- **Dynamic Evaluation**: Regularly review and update the risk impact assessments to reflect new developments or information in the project.

- **Responsive Strategies**: Be prepared to adjust risk management strategies and responses as the understanding of risk impact evolves.

Conclusion

Assessing and documenting the consequences and impact of risks is vital for understanding their potential effects on a project. This process involves a thorough evaluation of both direct and indirect impacts, consulting with stakeholders, and prioritizing risks based on their severity. Accurate documentation and regular updates of these assessments are crucial for developing effective risk responses and ensuring the project remains aligned with its objectives.

EMPOWERMENT OF STAKEHOLDERS TO CHALLENGE EXISTING RISK THRESHOLDS

Empowering stakeholders to challenge existing thresholds in risk management is a strategic approach that promotes critical thinking and proactive involvement. It helps ensure that risk thresholds are continually aligned with the evolving project environment and stakeholder needs. Here's how to facilitate this empowerment:

1. Educate Stakeholders on Risk Thresholds

- **Understanding Thresholds**: Provide stakeholders with clear explanations of what risk thresholds are and how they are determined. This includes thresholds for costs, time, quality, and other project metrics.

- **Training Sessions**: Conduct training sessions or workshops to deepen stakeholders' understanding of risk management principles, including threshold setting.

2. Foster a Culture of Open Communication

- **Encourage Open Dialogue**: Create an environment where stakeholders feel comfortable voicing concerns and suggestions regarding current risk thresholds.

- **Regular Meetings**: Hold regular meetings or forums where stakeholders can discuss and review risk thresholds.

3. Involve Stakeholders in Threshold Setting

- **Collaborative Reviews**: Involve stakeholders in the review process of existing thresholds, encouraging them to provide input based on their expertise and perspective.

- **Decision-Making Process**: Include stakeholders in the decision-making process when setting or adjusting risk thresholds.

4. Create Channels for Feedback and Suggestions

- **Feedback Mechanisms**: Establish clear channels through which stakeholders can provide feedback or challenge existing thresholds, such as suggestion boxes, dedicated email addresses, or regular surveys.

- **Responsiveness**: Ensure that there is a process in place to respond to and act upon the feedback received.

5. Acknowledge and Address Concerns

- **Consideration of Views**: Actively consider and address stakeholder concerns about risk thresholds. This might involve re-evaluating and adjusting thresholds where justified.

- **Transparency**: Be transparent about how stakeholder feedback is being used to influence risk threshold adjustments.

6. Support Data-Driven Decision Making

- **Provide Access to Data**: Give stakeholders access to relevant data and analysis tools to help them understand why certain thresholds are set and to formulate informed challenges or suggestions.

- **Data Interpretation Support**: Offer support in interpreting data related to risk thresholds, such as trends in risk occurrences or impacts.

7. Recognize and Value Contributions

- **Acknowledgment**: Publicly acknowledge and value the contributions of stakeholders who actively participate in challenging and refining risk thresholds.

- **Reward Constructive Challenges**: Consider recognizing constructive challenges and useful feedback, reinforcing a culture of proactive engagement.

Conclusion

Empowering stakeholders to challenge existing thresholds is about creating an environment of continuous improvement in risk management. It involves educating stakeholders, encouraging open communication, involving them in decision-making, and valuing their contributions. This approach not only leads to more robust and relevant risk thresholds but also enhances stakeholder buy-in and commitment to the project's success.

CASE STUDY: RENEWABLE ENERGY PROJECT

Context

An energy company is launching a renewable energy project involving the construction of wind farms and solar panels. In this dynamic and environmentally sensitive context, documenting risk triggers and thresholds is crucial for successful project execution and compliance with regulatory and environmental standards.

Assessing and Confirming Risk Compliance Thresholds

- **Compliance Thresholds**: Reviewing environmental regulations, safety standards, and industry best practices to establish compliance thresholds.

- **Updated Risk Data:** Utilizing recent data on environmental impact, technological advancements, and stakeholder feedback to reassess these thresholds.

- **Documentation:** Creating a comprehensive document outlining all compliance thresholds and how they align with current risk data.

Documenting Risk Triggers, Causes, and Timing

- **Risk Triggers:** Identifying specific events or conditions that could trigger risks, such as extreme weather events impacting construction timelines.

- **Causes:** Understanding the underlying causes of these risks, like climate change increasing the frequency of extreme weather.

- **Timing:** Assessing when these risks are most likely to occur during the project lifecycle.

Assessing and Documenting Risk Consequences/Impact

- **Risk Consequences:** Evaluating the potential impact of each identified risk on project objectives, such as delays, increased costs, or environmental damage.

- **Impact Analysis:** Documenting the severity of impact for each risk, considering both immediate and long-term consequences.

Empowering Stakeholders to Challenge Existing Thresholds

- **Stakeholder Workshops:** Conducting workshops where stakeholders can review and provide input on the established risk thresholds.

- **Feedback Mechanism:** Implementing a system for stakeholders to continuously provide feedback and challenge risk thresholds as the project progresses.

- **Adaptability:** Ensuring that the risk management plan is adaptable, allowing for revisions based on stakeholder input and changing environmental conditions.

Conclusion

In the renewable energy project, documenting risk triggers and thresholds based on the specific context and environment is a vital part of risk management. By assessing, confirming, and documenting compliance thresholds, triggers, causes, timing, and consequences of risks, the project risk manager establishes a clear understanding of the risk landscape. Empowering stakeholders to challenge and provide feedback on these thresholds ensures that the risk management approach remains dynamic and responsive to changing conditions. This structured and participative approach aligns with PMI standards and is essential in managing risks effectively in environmentally sensitive and technologically evolving projects like renewable energy developments.

Task 4 Develop risk register

ANALYSIS OF THE VALIDITY OF IDENTIFIED RISKS AND THEIR TRIGGERS

Analyzing the validity of identified risks and triggers is an essential step in developing a risk register. This process involves evaluating whether the identified risks are relevant and realistic, and confirming that the triggers are accurate indicators of potential risk occurrence. Here's how to approach this analysis:

1. Review Identified Risks and Triggers

- **Compilation**: Begin by compiling a comprehensive list of all identified risks and their associated triggers, gathered from various risk identification exercises.

- **Initial Assessment**: Conduct an initial assessment to ensure that each listed risk and trigger is clearly defined and understood.

2. Evaluate Relevance and Realism

- **Contextual Relevance**: Assess whether each risk is relevant to the specific context of the project. Ensure that the risks align with the project's scope, objectives, and environment.

- **Realism Check**: Evaluate the realism of each risk. Determine if the risk is a genuine possibility given the project's parameters and constraints.

3. Confirm Accuracy of Triggers

- **Trigger Association**: Verify that each trigger is accurately associated with its corresponding risk. Confirm that the occurrence of the trigger would likely indicate the onset of the risk.

- **Trigger Validity**: Ensure that triggers are valid indicators and not merely hypothetical or too vague.

4. Consult with Subject Matter Experts (SMEs) and Stakeholders

- **Expert Insights**: Engage SMEs and stakeholders to gain their perspectives on the identified risks and triggers. They can provide insights based on their expertise and experience.

- **Validation through Discussion**: Use meetings or workshops to discuss and validate the identified risks and triggers with these groups.

5. Analyze Historical Data

- **Past Projects and Trends**: Review historical data from similar projects or industry trends to determine if the identified risks and triggers have precedent and are based on factual occurrences.

6. Cross-Referencing with Project Documentation

- **Documentation Review**: Cross-reference risks and triggers with existing project documentation, such as the project plan, scope statement, and resource allocation documents, to ensure consistency and alignment.

7. Document Findings

- **Detailed Documentation**: Document the outcomes of the validity analysis in the risk register. Include notes on how each risk and trigger was validated and any relevant insights from SMEs, stakeholders, and historical data.

8. Regular Updates and Reassessment

- **Dynamic Process**: Treat the validation of risks and triggers as a dynamic process. Regularly revisit and reassess the risks and triggers to ensure they remain valid throughout the project lifecycle.

Conclusion

Analyzing the validity of identified risks and triggers is crucial for ensuring that the risk register is accurate and reflective of the actual risk landscape of the project. This process requires careful examination, consultation with experts and stakeholders, and continual reassessment to maintain its relevance and effectiveness.

EXAMINATION OF RISK ATTRIBUTES INCLUDING PROBABILITY, IMPACT, AND URGENCY

Examining the risk attributes like probability, impact, and urgency is a critical part of risk analysis in project management. These attributes help in understanding the nature of each risk and guide the development of appropriate risk response strategies. Here's a structured approach to examining these attributes:

1. Assessing Probability

- **Definition**: Probability is the likelihood of a risk occurring. It is typically assessed on a scale (e.g., low, medium, high) or as a percentage.

- **Factors to Consider**: Evaluate factors such as past occurrences, expert judgments, and current project conditions to estimate the probability of each risk.

- **Quantitative and Qualitative Analysis**: Use both qualitative assessments (like expert opinion) and quantitative methods (like statistical analysis) for probability estimation.

2. Evaluating Impact

- **Definition**: Impact refers to the potential effect a risk would have on the project if it materializes. It can affect various aspects like project scope, schedule, budget, and quality.

- **Scale of Impact**: Assess the impact using a predefined scale (e.g., low, medium, high) or specific metrics (like cost or time overrun).

- **Multiple Scenarios**: Consider different scenarios to understand the range of possible impacts for each risk.

3. Determining Urgency

- **Definition**: Urgency is the measure of how quickly a response is needed for a particular risk. It depends on factors like risk velocity and the time window available to respond effectively.

- **Assessment of Response Time**: Evaluate how much time is available to respond to the risk and how quickly the risk could impact the project.

- **Prioritization Based on Urgency**: Prioritize risks that require immediate attention or intervention.

4. Documenting Risk Attributes

- **Risk Register Entries**: Document the assessments of probability, impact, and urgency for each risk in the risk register.

- **Detailed Descriptions**: Provide clear explanations for the ratings given, including any assumptions or data sources used in the assessment.

5. Stakeholder Consultation

- **Expert Input**: Consult with project stakeholders and subject matter experts to validate or adjust the assessments of probability, impact, and urgency.

- **Feedback Integration**: Incorporate feedback from these consultations to refine the risk assessments.

6. Regular Review and Update

- **Dynamic Assessment**: Regularly review and update the assessments of risk attributes to reflect any changes in the project environment or new information.

- **Adaptability**: Be prepared to adapt risk management strategies based on updated assessments.

Conclusion

Examining and documenting the attributes of probability, impact, and urgency for each risk are fundamental to effective risk management. This process requires a careful balance of expert judgment, historical data analysis, and stakeholder consultation. Regular reviews and updates of these attributes ensure that the risk management approach remains relevant and responsive to the project's evolving needs.

ESTABLISHMENT OF RISK ORIGIN AND OWNERSHIP

Establishing risk origin and ownership is a crucial step in risk management, as it helps in identifying the source of risks and assigning responsibility for managing them. Understanding whether a risk is internal or external is important for developing appropriate response strategies. Here's how to approach this:

1. Identifying Risk Origin

- **Internal Risks**: These are risks that originate within the project or organization. They could be related to processes, resources, personnel, or technology. For example, a risk could stem from internal operational inefficiencies or resource constraints.

- **External Risks**: External risks arise from outside the project or organization. They include market fluctuations, regulatory changes, natural disasters, or actions by competitors.

2. Assessing Risk Characteristics

- **Analysis of Causes**: Analyze each identified risk to understand its root causes and whether these are internal or external.

- **Contextual Factors**: Consider the broader project and organizational context to accurately determine the risk origin.

3. Assigning Risk Ownership

- **Responsibility Assignment**: Assign a risk owner for each identified risk. The owner is typically someone who has the authority, knowledge, and capacity to manage the risk.

- **Ownership Criteria**: Choose owners based on their ability to influence or control the risk. For internal risks, owners are usually within the project team or organization. For external risks, consider assigning someone who can closely monitor and respond to external conditions.

4. Documenting Risk Origin and Ownership

- **Risk Register**: Document the origin and ownership of each risk in the risk register. Include details about the nature of the risk and the rationale for the assigned ownership.

- **Clear Descriptions**: Provide clear and concise descriptions to ensure that the origin and ownership are well-understood by all stakeholders.

5. Communication and Accountability

- **Stakeholder Communication**: Communicate the risk origins and ownership assignments to all relevant stakeholders.

- **Accountability**: Ensure that risk owners understand their responsibilities and the expectations for managing their respective risks.

6. Training and Support for Risk Owners

- **Owner Empowerment**: Provide training and support to risk owners, especially in areas such as risk response planning and monitoring.

- **Resources and Authority**: Ensure that risk owners have the necessary resources and authority to effectively manage their risks.

7. Regular Reviews and Adjustments

- **Review of Assignments**: Regularly review risk origin and ownership assignments to ensure they remain relevant and effective.

- **Flexibility for Changes**: Be prepared to adjust assignments as the project progresses or as new information comes to light.

Conclusion

Establishing the origin and ownership of risks is essential for effective risk management. It involves a detailed analysis of each risk, clear documentation, and the assignment of responsibility to appropriate individuals. Effective communication, regular reviews, and ongoing support for risk owners are key to ensuring that risks are managed proactively and effectively throughout the project lifecycle.

CLASSIFICATION OF RISKS AS THREATS OR OPPORTUNITIES

Classifying risks as threats or opportunities is a fundamental aspect of risk management, which allows for a more nuanced approach to dealing with potential uncertainties in a project. This classification helps in identifying not just the risks that could negatively impact the project, but also those that could present potential benefits. Here's how to approach this classification:

1. Understanding the Nature of Risks

- **Threats**: These are risks that, if they occur, will have a negative impact on the project, potentially harming its objectives, such as delays, cost overruns, or quality issues.

- **Opportunities**: These are risks that, if they occur, will have a positive impact on the project, potentially enhancing its value, efficiency, or effectiveness.

2. Analyzing Each Identified Risk

- **Assess the Impact**: Evaluate the potential impact of each identified risk. Determine whether the impact is negative (threat) or positive (opportunity).

- **Consider Contextual Factors**: Analyze the specific circumstances of the project to understand how each risk could play out in that context.

3. Consulting with Stakeholders and Experts

- **Stakeholder Insights**: Engage with various stakeholders and subject matter experts to gain their perspectives on the nature of each risk.

- **Collective Assessment**: Use the collective insights from these discussions to aid in the classification process.

4. Utilizing Risk Assessment Tools

- **Risk Matrices and SWOT Analysis**: Use tools like risk matrices or SWOT (Strengths, Weaknesses, Opportunities, Threats) analysis to help categorize risks.

- **Quantitative Methods**: For more complex risks, consider quantitative methods like scenario analysis or probabilistic modeling.

5. Documenting Risk Classifications

- **Risk Register Entries**: In the risk register, clearly document the classification of each risk as either a threat or an opportunity.

- **Rationale for Classification**: Include the rationale behind the classification, detailing the expected impact and the basis for determining it as a threat or opportunity.

6. Review and Reassess Classifications

- **Regular Reviews**: Regularly review the risk classifications to ensure they remain accurate and relevant, as risks can evolve over the lifecycle of a project.

- **Be Open to Re-classification**: Be prepared to reclassify risks as new information emerges or as the project environment changes.

7. Developing Appropriate Strategies

- **Response Planning**: For threats, develop mitigation or avoidance strategies. For opportunities, develop strategies to capture or enhance the positive impacts.

- **Incorporate into Risk Management Plan**: Ensure that the strategies for both threats and opportunities are integrated into the overall risk management plan.

Conclusion

Classifying risks as threats or opportunities enables a more strategic approach to risk management, allowing project teams to mitigate potential problems and capitalize on potential benefits. It involves a careful analysis of each risk, consultation with stakeholders, and documentation in the risk register. Regular review and adaptability in classification are crucial as the project progresses and new information becomes available.

CASE STUDY: HIGH-SPEED RAIL CONSTRUCTION PROJECT

Context

A national transportation authority is undertaking a high-speed rail construction project. This complex and high-profile project requires meticulous risk management. Developing a comprehensive risk register is a crucial step in this process.

Analyzing the Validity of Identified Risks and Triggers

- **Risk Validation:** Reviewing each identified risk to ensure they are relevant and current to the project's context.

- **Trigger Analysis:** Examining the triggers for each risk to understand the conditions or events that could cause the risk to materialize.

Examining Risk Attributes

- **Probability:** Assessing the likelihood of each risk occurring during the project lifecycle.

- **Impact:** Evaluating the potential effect of the risk on project objectives, such as budget, schedule, safety, and quality.

- **Urgency:** Determining the time sensitivity of each risk and the need for immediate action or monitoring.

Establishing Risk Origin and Ownership

- **Risk Origin:** Identifying whether each risk is internal (originating within the project, such as resource constraints) or external (originating outside the project, like regulatory changes).

- **Ownership Assignment:** Allocating each risk to a specific owner within the project team who will be responsible for monitoring and managing the risk.

Classifying Risks as Threats or Opportunities

- **Threats:** Identifying risks that could negatively impact the project, such as delays due to land acquisition issues or cost overruns due to material price increases.

- **Opportunities:** Recognizing potential positive risks that could benefit the project, like the availability of new, more efficient construction technologies or opportunities for cost savings.

Conclusion

For the high-speed rail construction project, the development of the risk register is a critical task that involves a thorough analysis and categorization of risks. By validating identified risks and triggers, examining their attributes, establishing their origins and ownership, and classifying them as threats or opportunities, the project risk manager creates a robust tool for effective risk management. This risk register not only aids in the proactive management of potential challenges but also in capitalizing on opportunities, aligning with PMI standards for risk management in large-scale infrastructure projects. This comprehensive approach ensures that risks are well-understood and effectively managed throughout the project lifecycle.

DOMAIN III
RISK ANALYSIS

Task 1 Perform qualitative analysis

NOMINAL CLASSIFICATION OF RISKS IN THE RISK BREAKDOWN STRUCTURE (RBS)

Performing a nominal classification of risks in the Risk Breakdown Structure (RBS) using classifications from the risk management plan is a key step in qualitative risk analysis. This process involves categorizing identified risks into various predefined areas to facilitate a structured and systematic approach to risk analysis. Here's how to approach this task:

1. Review the Risk Management Plan

- **Understand Classifications**: Start by reviewing the risk management plan to understand the established risk classifications. Typical classifications include environmental, organizational, project management, technical, and more.

- **Alignment with RBS**: Ensure that these classifications align with the categories defined in the Risk Breakdown Structure (RBS).

2. Organize Risks in the RBS

- **Risk Breakdown Structure**: Use the RBS as a framework for categorizing risks. The RBS should be a hierarchical representation of potential sources of risk in the project.

- **Categorization**: Assign each identified risk to the appropriate category in the RBS. For example, risks related to weather conditions would fall under the 'environmental' category, while risks related to staffing would be under 'organizational'.

3. Nominal Classification Process

- **Discrete Categories**: Classify each risk into discrete categories as per the RBS. This classification is nominal, meaning it is based on naming or labeling the types of risks.

- **Avoid Overlapping**: Ensure that each risk is placed in the most relevant category, avoiding overlaps where possible.

4. Documenting the Classification

- **Risk Register Entries**: Document the classification of each risk in the risk register, alongside its description and other relevant details.

- **Clear Justification**: Provide justification for why each risk has been categorized as such, especially if a risk could potentially fit into multiple categories.

5. Review and Validation

- **Stakeholder Consultation**: Engage with stakeholders and subject matter experts to review and validate the risk classifications. Their insights might lead to re-categorization or identification of additional risks.

- **Iterative Process**: Treat the classification as an iterative process, revisiting and adjusting it as new information emerges.

6. Utilize for Further Analysis

- **Foundation for Analysis**: Use these classifications as a foundation for further qualitative and quantitative risk analysis, such as prioritizing risks within each category or performing deeper impact assessments.

7. Training and Communication

- **Stakeholder Training**: Train stakeholders on the nominal classification system used in the RBS to ensure consistency in how risks are categorized and understood.

- **Effective Communication**: Communicate the categorized risks to the project team and relevant stakeholders, ensuring they understand the categorization logic and its implications for risk management.

Conclusion

Nominal classification of risks in the RBS is a methodical approach that enhances the organization and understanding of risks. It serves as a basis for deeper risk analysis and management activities. This process requires careful consideration of the risk management plan's categories, thorough documentation, and regular stakeholder engagement for validation and refinement.

ESTIMATION OF RISK IMPACT ON PROJECT SCHEDULE, BUDGET, RESOURCES, AND SCOPE

Estimating the impact of risk on project schedule, budget, resources, and scope is a fundamental part of qualitative risk analysis. This estimation helps in understanding how potential risks could affect key aspects of a project and aids in prioritizing risks for response planning. Here's a structured approach to estimate these impacts:

1. Estimating Impact on Project Schedule

- **Identify Risks Affecting Schedule**: Determine which risks could lead to delays or accelerations in the project timeline.

- **Assess Duration Impact**: Evaluate how much each identified risk could extend or shorten the project schedule. Use tools like Gantt charts or critical path analysis to assess the potential delay.

- **Consider Dependencies**: Account for how risks might affect dependent tasks or milestones in the project.

2. Estimating Impact on Budget

- **Risks Affecting Costs**: Identify risks that could lead to increased costs, such as price fluctuations, unexpected resource needs, or overtime work.

- **Quantify Cost Changes**: Estimate the potential increase or decrease in costs due to each risk. Consider using historical data or expert judgment for more accurate estimations.

Alexander Stratton

- **Contingency Planning**: Include potential cost impacts in the project's contingency planning.

3. Estimating Impact on Resources

- **Resource Risks**: Identify risks related to workforce availability, equipment, materials, or other necessary resources.
- **Resource Availability and Usage**: Assess how each risk could affect the availability or usage rate of resources. Consider potential shortages, over-allocations, or efficiencies.
- **Alternative Resource Plans**: Plan for alternative resource solutions in case the risk materializes.

4. Estimating Impact on Project Scope

- **Scope-Related Risks**: Pinpoint risks that could lead to changes in project scope, such as scope creep, specification changes, or external factors forcing scope adjustments.
- **Scope Change Assessment**: Determine how these risks might expand or contract the project scope. Assess the likelihood of additional work or the need to reduce deliverables.
- **Stakeholder Expectations**: Consider how scope changes could impact stakeholder expectations and satisfaction.

5. Documenting the Impact Assessments

- **Detailed Documentation**: Record the estimated impacts of risks on schedule, budget, resources, and scope in the risk register or a separate risk analysis document.
- **Rationale and Data Sources**: Include the rationale behind each estimation and any data sources or methodologies used.

6. Regular Review and Update

- **Dynamic Assessments**: Regularly review and update the impact assessments to reflect new information or changes in the project environment.
- **Adaptability in Planning**: Be prepared to adapt project plans and strategies based on updated impact assessments.

Conclusion

Estimating the impact of risks on key project elements like schedule, budget, resources, and scope is essential for effective risk management. It involves a thorough analysis of potential risk effects and careful documentation. Regular

144

reviews and updates to these estimations ensure that risk management strategies remain relevant and effective throughout the project lifecycle.

PRIORITIZATION OF RISKS BASED ON IMPACT AND URGENCY

Prioritizing risks based on their impact and urgency is a critical step in risk management. This process helps in identifying which risks require immediate attention and resources, and which can be monitored over time. Here's a structured approach to prioritizing risks:

1. Assessing Risk Impact

- **Impact Evaluation**: Evaluate the potential impact of each identified risk on the project's objectives, such as scope, schedule, budget, and quality.

- **Quantitative and Qualitative Assessment**: Use both qualitative methods (like expert judgment) and quantitative methods (such as cost-benefit analysis) to assess impact.

- **Impact Scale**: Develop a scale to rate the impact of risks, typically ranging from low to high.

2. Determining Risk Urgency

- **Urgency Assessment**: Assess how quickly a response is required for each risk. Consider factors like risk velocity and the time window for effective response.

- **Time-Sensitive Risks**: Identify risks that are time-sensitive and require immediate action to prevent escalation.

3. Creating a Risk Prioritization Matrix

- **Risk Matrix Development**: Use a risk matrix to plot risks based on their impact and urgency. This visual tool helps in understanding the relative priority of each risk.

- **Matrix Quadrants**: Divide the matrix into quadrants (e.g., high impact/high urgency, high impact/low urgency, low impact/high urgency, low impact/low urgency) to categorize risks.

4. Ranking Risks

- **Prioritization**: Rank the risks within each quadrant of the matrix. Higher impact and more urgent risks should be given higher priority.

- **Focus on Critical Risks**: Pay particular attention to risks in the high impact/high urgency quadrant, as these are critical risks that require immediate attention.

5. Documenting and Communicating Priorities

- **Risk Register Update**: Document the prioritization of risks in the risk register, including the rationale behind the prioritization.

- **Stakeholder Communication**: Communicate the prioritized risks to relevant stakeholders, ensuring they are aware of and understand the prioritization.

6. Regular Review and Adjustment

- **Dynamic Prioritization**: Regularly review and adjust the prioritization of risks to reflect any changes in the project environment or new information.

- **Flexibility in Response Planning**: Be prepared to adjust risk response plans based on changes in risk prioritization.

Conclusion

Prioritizing risks based on impact and urgency is essential for efficient risk management. It allows project managers to allocate resources and attention effectively, focusing on the most critical risks. The use of a risk matrix aids in this process, providing a clear visual representation of risk priorities. Regular reviews and effective communication with stakeholders are key to maintaining an accurate and responsive risk prioritization strategy.

APPLICATION OF RISK MATRICES IN RISK ASSESSMENT

Applying risk matrices in risk management is an effective way to visualize and prioritize risks based on their probability and impact. A risk matrix helps in making informed decisions about which risks to focus on and how to allocate resources. Here's a guide on how to apply risk matrices effectively:

1. Developing the Risk Matrix

- **Matrix Structure**: Create a grid with probability on one axis (usually vertical) and impact on the other (usually horizontal). Each axis should be divided into categories like low, medium, and high.

- **Definitions of Probability and Impact**: Clearly define what each level of probability and impact means. For example, 'high probability' might be defined as a greater than 70% chance of occurring, while 'high impact' might involve significant cost overruns or major delays.

2. Agreed-Upon Assessment Approach

- **Consensus on Methodology**: Ensure there is an agreed-upon approach for assessing risks. This involves how probability and impact are measured and the criteria for categorizing risks on the matrix.

- **Stakeholder Alignment**: Align with all stakeholders on the chosen approach to ensure consistency and buy-in.

3. Utilizing Historical Information

- **Leverage Past Data**: Use historical data and information from past projects to inform the probability and impact assessments. This can provide a realistic basis for your evaluations.

- **Learning from Experience**: Analyze historical successes and failures to refine your risk assessment approach.

4. Categorizing Risks

- **Risk Categories**: Classify risks into categories (e.g., technical, operational, financial, environmental) before placing them on the matrix. This helps in understanding the nature of risks and potential response strategies.

- **Placement on Matrix**: Place each categorized risk on the matrix according to its assessed probability and impact.

5. Pre-Established Criteria

- **Criteria for Categorization**: Use pre-established criteria for determining where on the matrix a risk should fall. This ensures objectivity and consistency in the risk assessment process.

- **Thresholds for Action**: Establish thresholds or criteria for action based on the risk's position on the matrix (e.g., immediate action for high probability/high impact risks).

6. Review and Update

- **Regular Reviews**: Continually review and update the risk matrix as the project progresses and as new information comes to light.

- **Dynamic Adjustments**: Be prepared to move risks around on the matrix as their probability or impact changes.

7. Documentation and Communication

- **Document the Process**: Document the methodology, definitions, and criteria used in the risk matrix, as well as the placement of risks on the matrix.

- **Communicate with Stakeholders**: Share the risk matrix with stakeholders, providing them with a clear visual representation of risk prioritization.

Conclusion

A risk matrix is a valuable tool in risk management, providing a clear and visual representation of risks based on their probability and impact. It is essential to have clear definitions, agreed-upon assessment methodologies, and use historical data for accurate risk placement. Regular reviews and updates, along with clear documentation and communication, are crucial for the effective use of a risk matrix in managing project risks.

EXECUTION OF ORDINAL RISK CLASSIFICATION

Performing an ordinal classification of risks in project management involves ranking or ordering risks based on their severity, magnitude, or priority. Unlike nominal classification, which categorizes risks into different types without a specific order, ordinal classification arranges risks in a sequence that typically reflects their relative importance or urgency. Here's how to approach this:

1. Establish Criteria for Ranking

- **Define Ranking Factors**: Establish the factors based on which the risks will be ranked. Common factors include the impact of the risk, likelihood of occurrence, and urgency for response.

- **Consistency in Criteria**: Ensure that the criteria are applied consistently across all identified risks for an objective assessment.

2. Review and Assess Risks

- **Individual Risk Assessment**: Assess each identified risk based on the established criteria. Use information from qualitative and quantitative analyses, such as impact and probability assessments.

- **Relative Comparison**: Compare risks against each other to determine their relative importance or severity.

3. Ranking Risks

- **Sequential Ordering**: Arrange the risks in order, from the highest to the lowest, based on the assessment. For example, a risk with a high impact and high probability would rank higher than one with a lower impact and probability.

- **Use of Scales**: Apply numerical scales or descriptive labels (e.g., high, medium, low) for ease of understanding and communication.

4. Documenting the Ordinal Classification

- **Update Risk Register**: Document the ordinal classification of risks in the risk register or a separate risk analysis document.

- **Clear Justification**: Provide a rationale for the ranking of each risk, detailing the basis on which they were classified.

5. Stakeholder Consultation and Validation

- **Engage Stakeholders**: Consult with project stakeholders to validate the ordinal classification. Stakeholder insights can provide a different perspective and might lead to re-ranking.

- **Incorporate Feedback**: Adjust the risk rankings based on stakeholder feedback and additional information.

6. Use in Risk Management Planning

- **Prioritization for Responses**: Use the ordinal classification to prioritize risks for response planning. Higher-ranked risks might require more immediate and comprehensive response strategies.

- **Resource Allocation**: Allocate resources and attention in accordance with the risk ranking, focusing on higher-ranked risks first.

7. Regular Review and Update

- **Dynamic Process**: Treat the ordinal classification as a dynamic process. Regularly review and update the rankings as new risks emerge and as existing risks evolve.

Conclusion

Ordinal classification is a useful approach in risk management for prioritizing risks based on their relative importance or urgency. It involves a systematic assessment and ranking of risks, taking into account factors such as impact, likelihood, and urgency. Effective documentation, stakeholder engagement and regular reviews are key to ensuring that the ordinal classification remains relevant and useful throughout the project lifecycle.

COACHING STAKEHOLDERS ON RISK CATEGORIZATION STRATEGIES

Coaching stakeholders on risk categorization strategies is a vital task in risk management, as it ensures that everyone involved in the project has a clear understanding of how to identify, assess, and categorize risks effectively. Effective coaching can lead to more accurate risk identification and a better-informed approach to managing those risks. Here's a structured approach to coaching stakeholders:

1. Introduce the Basics of Risk Management

- **Explain Risk Concepts**: Start with the basics of risk management, explaining what risks are and why they are important to identify and manage in the context of a project.

- **Importance of Categorization**: Stress the importance of categorizing risks for effective analysis and response planning.

2. Discuss Different Categorization Methods

- **Nominal Classification**: Explain how to categorize risks based on types or nature, such as technical, financial, legal, or operational risks.

- **Ordinal Classification**: Teach stakeholders how to rank risks based on their severity or priority, such as high, medium, or low.

- **Risk Matrices**: Demonstrate how to use risk matrices to categorize risks by their probability and impact.

3. Provide Real-World Examples

- **Case Studies**: Use real-world examples or case studies to illustrate how different categorization strategies are applied in practice.

- **Lessons Learned**: Share lessons learned from past projects to highlight the importance of effective risk categorization.

4. Interactive Training Sessions

- **Workshops**: Conduct interactive workshops where stakeholders can practice categorizing different types of risks.

- **Group Activities**: Use group activities to encourage collaboration and discussion among stakeholders on risk categorization.

5. Use of Tools and Software

- **Demonstrate Tools**: If specific tools or software are used for risk categorization, provide demonstrations on how to use them.

- **Hands-on Practice**: Allow stakeholders to practice using these tools during training sessions.

6. Encourage Questions and Discussion

- **Open Q&A Sessions**: Hold open question-and-answer sessions where stakeholders can ask questions and clarify doubts.

- **Encourage Participation**: Foster an environment where stakeholders feel comfortable discussing and sharing their perspectives on risk categorization.

7. Provide Supporting Materials

- **Handouts and Guides**: Provide handouts, guides, or online resources that stakeholders can refer to after training sessions.

- **Ongoing Support**: Offer to provide ongoing support and answer questions as stakeholders apply these strategies in their roles.

8. Regular Follow-Up and Feedback

- **Check-Ins**: Conduct regular follow-ups to assess how stakeholders are applying their knowledge of risk categorization.

- **Feedback Mechanism**: Establish a mechanism for stakeholders to provide feedback on the training and its applicability to their roles.

Conclusion

Coaching stakeholders on risk categorization strategies is about providing them with the knowledge, tools, and confidence to effectively categorize risks. Through interactive training, real-world examples, and ongoing support, stakeholders can develop a solid understanding of how to categorize risks accurately and contribute effectively to the project's risk management process.

CASE STUDY: HEALTHCARE SYSTEM MODERNIZATION PROJECT

Context

A healthcare organization is undertaking a project to modernize its healthcare systems, including upgrading patient record systems and implementing new telehealth services. Performing a qualitative risk analysis is crucial to assess and prioritize risks associated with this complex project.

Performing a Nominal Classification of Risks in the RBS

- **Risk Breakdown Structure (RBS):** Developing an RBS that categorizes risks into areas such as environmental, organizational, project management, and technical.

- **Nominal Classification:** Assigning each identified risk to a category within the RBS based on the nature and source of the risk.

Estimating the Impact of Risk on Project Schedule, Budget, Resources, and Scope

- **Schedule Impact:** Assessing how risks could delay project milestones, such as implementation deadlines.

- **Budget Impact:** Evaluating the potential for cost overruns due to risks like technology procurement delays or unexpected regulatory compliance costs.

- **Resource Impact:** Analyzing risks associated with workforce availability, technology resources, and vendor support.

- **Scope Impact:** Considering risks that might necessitate changes to the project scope, like evolving healthcare regulations.

Prioritizing the Risk Based on Impact and Urgency

- **Impact Assessment:** Determining how significantly each risk could affect the project's objectives.

- **Urgency Evaluation:** Identifying which risks require immediate attention and which can be monitored over time.

Applying Risk Matrices

- **Assessment Approach:** Utilizing a risk matrix with agreed-upon approaches, historical information, and pre-established criteria.

- **Probability and Impact Definitions:** Defining clear criteria for the probability of occurrence and potential impact of each risk.

- **Risk Categorization:** Applying the matrix to categorize risks based on their assessed probability and impact.

Performing an Ordinal Classification

- **Ranking Risks:** Ordering risks based on their priority, determined by their impact and urgency.

- **Ordinal Scale:** Using a scale (such as high, medium, low) to classify and communicate the relative importance of each risk.

Coaching Stakeholders on Risk Categorization Strategies

- **Training Sessions:** Conducting workshops and training sessions to educate stakeholders on risk categorization methodologies.

- **Guidance Materials:** Providing materials that explain the risk categorization process, including the use of risk matrices and RBS.

- **Interactive Exercises:** Engaging stakeholders in exercises to practice risk categorization and prioritization.

Conclusion

In the healthcare system modernization project, performing a qualitative risk analysis involves a systematic approach to categorizing, assessing, and prioritizing risks. By using tools like the RBS and risk matrices, and by coaching stakeholders in these methodologies, the project risk manager ensures that risks are comprehensively analyzed and effectively communicated. This approach not only aligns with PMI standards but also ensures that stakeholders are actively engaged and informed, thereby enhancing the project's ability to navigate risks in a dynamic healthcare environment. The qualitative risk analysis serves as a foundation for proactive risk management, contributing to the project's overall success.

Task 2 Perform quantitative analysis

ANALYSIS OF RISK DATA AND PROCESS PERFORMANCE AGAINST ESTABLISHED METRICS

Analyzing risk data and process performance information against established metrics is a key component of quantitative risk analysis in project management. This process involves comparing collected risk data and performance indicators to predefined standards or benchmarks to gauge the severity and implications of risks. Here's how to approach this task:

1. Gather Risk Data and Performance Information

- **Collect Data**: Assemble all relevant risk data and information on process performance. This can include data on risk occurrences, impact, frequency, and any changes in risk status.

- **Performance Metrics**: Gather data on key performance indicators (KPIs) of the project, such as schedule adherence, budget performance, quality metrics, and resource utilization.

2. Identify Established Metrics

- **Define Benchmarks**: Identify the established metrics or benchmarks against which the risk data and performance information will be analyzed. These could be industry standards, historical project data, or specific targets set for the project.

- **Ensure Relevance**: Confirm that the established metrics are relevant and appropriate for the type of risks and performance aspects being measured.

3. Analyze Against Metrics

- **Comparative Analysis**: Compare the collected risk and performance data against the established metrics. This involves looking for deviations, trends, and patterns that indicate risk impacts.

- **Quantitative Techniques**: Use quantitative techniques such as statistical analysis, trend analysis, and variance analysis to interpret the data.

4. Interpreting Findings

- **Assess Implications**: Interpret the results to understand the implications of the findings. Determine if the risks are within acceptable limits or if they are impacting the project's performance adversely.

- **Contextual Understanding**: Consider the context of the project when interpreting the data, as different projects might have different risk tolerances and performance expectations.

5. Document and Report Findings

- **Detailed Documentation**: Document the findings of the analysis in a detailed report, including how the data compares to the established metrics.

- **Visualization**: Use charts, graphs, and tables to visualize the data, making it easier to understand and communicate the findings.

6. Stakeholder Communication

- **Share Results**: Communicate the results of the analysis with relevant stakeholders, including project team members, management, and clients.

- **Feedback and Discussion**: Encourage feedback and discussion on the findings to gain different perspectives and insights.

7. Informing Decision-Making

- **Risk Response Planning**: Use the insights gained from the analysis to inform risk response planning. Adjust strategies based on how risks are impacting performance relative to the metrics.

- **Continuous Improvement**: Apply the findings for continuous improvement in risk management and project execution processes.

Conclusion

Analyzing risk data and process performance information against established metrics is crucial for quantitatively understanding the impact of risks on a project. It provides a basis for making informed decisions about risk management strategies and for ongoing improvements in project performance. Effective documentation and clear communication of the findings are essential for transparency and stakeholder engagement in the risk management process.

COMPREHENSIVE ANALYSIS OF A PROJECT'S GENERAL RISKS

Analyzing a project's general risks involves a comprehensive review of potential uncertainties that could impact the project's overall success. This analysis is crucial for identifying, understanding, and preparing for various risks that might affect the project's objectives. Here's how to approach the analysis of general risks:

1. Identify Potential Risks

- **Brainstorming**: Conduct brainstorming sessions with the project team and other stakeholders to identify potential risks.

- **Review Project Documentation**: Analyze project plans, reports, and historical data for any indications of potential risks.

- **Expert Consultation**: Consult with subject matter experts who can provide insights into risks based on their experience and expertise.

2. Categorize Risks

- **Risk Categories**: Categorize the identified risks into relevant groups such as technical, financial, operational, environmental, and organizational risks.

- **Risk Breakdown Structure (RBS)**: Utilize an RBS to systematically categorize and structure the risks.

3. Assess Each Risk

- **Probability Assessment**: Evaluate the likelihood of each risk occurring. This can be done qualitatively (low, medium, high) or quantitatively (percentage likelihood).

- **Impact Assessment**: Determine the potential impact of each risk on the project. Consider aspects like schedule delays, cost overruns, and quality issues.

4. Prioritize Risks

- **Risk Matrix**: Use a risk matrix to prioritize risks based on their probability and impact. This helps in identifying which risks require immediate attention and resources.

- **Focus on High-Priority Risks**: Allocate more resources and planning efforts to manage risks that are both highly likely and have significant impacts.

5. Perform Qualitative and Quantitative Analysis

- **Qualitative Analysis**: Perform a qualitative analysis to get a broad understanding of the risks and their potential effects.

- **Quantitative Analysis**: Where necessary, conduct quantitative analyses such as sensitivity analysis, expected monetary value analysis, or Monte Carlo simulations for a more detailed risk assessment.

6. Develop Risk Responses

- **Response Strategies**: Develop response strategies for each prioritized risk, including mitigation, transfer, acceptance, or avoidance strategies.

- **Contingency Plans**: Create contingency plans for risks that might not be mitigated fully.

7. Document and Communicate the Analysis

- **Risk Register**: Document all identified risks, their assessments, and response plans in a risk register.

- **Stakeholder Communication**: Communicate the results of the risk analysis to stakeholders, ensuring they understand the potential risks and the plans in place to manage them.

8. Review and Update Regularly

- **Dynamic Process**: Treat risk analysis as a dynamic process. Regularly review and update the risk analysis to reflect new information or changes in the project environment.

Conclusion

Analyzing a project's general risks is an essential step in proactive risk management. It involves identifying, categorizing, assessing, and prioritizing risks, followed by planning appropriate response strategies. Effective communication, documentation, and regular updates are crucial to ensure that the risk management process remains relevant throughout the project lifecycle.

EXECUTION OF FORECAST AND TREND ANALYSIS USING NEW AND HISTORICAL INFORMATION

Performing a forecast and trend analysis on new and historical information is a critical component of quantitative risk analysis in project management. This process involves using past project data and current project information to predict future trends and potential risks. Here's a structured approach to conducting this analysis:

1. Gather Historical and Current Data

- **Historical Data**: Collect data from previous similar projects or phases. This can include project performance metrics, risk occurrences, and response effectiveness.

- **Current Project Data**: Gather current data related to the project's progress, including schedule adherence, budget status, resource utilization, and identified risks.

2. Analyze Historical Trends

- **Identify Patterns**: Look for patterns in the historical data, such as common types of risks, frequent causes of delays, or typical cost overruns.

- **Benchmarking**: Compare historical performance against industry benchmarks or standards to identify areas of risk or concern.

3. Apply Forecasting Methods

- **Time Series Analysis**: Use time series analysis to identify trends over time and forecast future project performance based on historical patterns.

- **Regression Analysis**: Apply regression analysis to understand the relationship between different variables (e.g., the impact of resource changes on project schedule).

4. Incorporate Current Project Information

- **Real-Time Data Analysis**: Analyze current project data to assess how the project is performing against planned metrics and forecasts.

- **Risk Event Tracking**: Track current risk events and responses to assess their impact on the project.

5. Perform Trend Analysis

- **Project Performance Trends**: Identify trends in project performance metrics, such as increasing costs or slipping schedules.

- **Risk Occurrence Trends**: Analyze trends in risk occurrence and impact to understand potential future risks.

6. Develop Forecasts

- **Predictive Models**: Use predictive modeling techniques to forecast future project performance and potential risks. Techniques may include Monte Carlo simulations, decision trees, or expected monetary value analysis.

- **Scenario Analysis**: Conduct scenario analysis to understand the potential impacts of different risk events or project changes.

7. Document and Communicate Findings

- **Reporting**: Document the results of the forecast and trend analysis in a comprehensive report. Include visual representations like graphs and charts to illustrate trends and forecasts.

- **Stakeholder Communication**: Communicate the findings to project stakeholders, providing insights into potential future risks and project performance.

8. Update Risk Management Plans

- **Inform Risk Response Strategies**: Use the insights gained from the forecast and trend analysis to update risk response plans and project management strategies.

- **Continuous Monitoring**: Establish a process for continuous monitoring of project performance and risks, updating forecasts and trends as new data becomes available.

Conclusion

Forecast and trend analysis provides valuable insights into potential future project performance and risks, allowing for proactive risk management and informed decision-making. It involves a detailed analysis of historical and current project data, application of various forecasting techniques, and effective communication of the findings to stakeholders. Regular updates and continuous monitoring are key to maintaining the relevance and accuracy of the forecasts and trends.

CONDUCTING SENSITIVITY ANALYSIS USING ADVANCED TECHNIQUES

Performing sensitivity analysis is a key aspect of quantitative risk analysis in project management. This process involves assessing how different uncertainties or scenarios affect a project's outcome. Common methods for sensitivity analysis include Monte Carlo simulations, decision trees, critical path analysis, and expected monetary value calculations. Here's a guide on how to use these methods:

1. Monte Carlo Simulations

- **Methodology**: Use Monte Carlo simulations to model the probability of different outcomes in a process that cannot easily be predicted due to the intervention of random variables.

- **Application**: Apply this method to project schedules or budgets by running simulations that vary key inputs (like task duration or cost) to see their impact on project completion dates or total costs.

- **Tool Usage**: Utilize specialized software that can perform these simulations and provide probabilistic results.

2. Decision Trees

- **Methodology**: Decision trees help in visualizing and analyzing decisions under uncertainty. They map out different decision paths and the likelihoods and outcomes of each path.

- **Application**: Use decision trees to evaluate choices in risk responses, such as choosing between different vendors, technologies, or project approaches.

- **Probability and Outcome Assessment**: For each branch of the tree, assign probabilities and potential outcomes (costs, benefits, timeframes).

3. Critical Path Analysis

- **Methodology**: Critical path analysis identifies the longest path of planned activities to the end of the project and the earliest and latest that each activity can start and finish without making the project longer.

- **Application**: Apply it to assess how delays in critical tasks will affect project deadlines.

- **Sensitivity Identification**: Identify which tasks have the least slack and are most sensitive to delays.

4. Expected Monetary Value Analysis

- **Methodology**: Expected Monetary Value (EMV) analysis is a statistical technique in risk management used to quantify risks by multiplying the value of each possible outcome by its probability of occurrence.

- **Application**: Use EMV to assess the overall financial impact of risks by considering both the probability of occurrences and the potential financial impact of each risk.

- **Risk Quantification**: Calculate the EMV for individual risks and then aggregate them to get a total expected value for the project.

5. Documenting the Analysis

- **Risk Register Update**: Document the findings and outcomes of the sensitivity analysis in the risk register.

- **Reporting**: Provide detailed reports on the sensitivity analysis to stakeholders, highlighting key risks and their potential impacts.

6. Incorporating into Risk Response Planning

- **Inform Strategies**: Use insights from the sensitivity analysis to inform risk response strategies. Focus on risks that have the greatest impact on key project objectives.

- **Resource Allocation**: Allocate resources and attention to managing the most sensitive risks.

Conclusion

Sensitivity analysis in project management involves a range of techniques to assess the impact of uncertainties on project outcomes. Each method provides a different perspective on risk, from probabilistic outcomes to decision impacts. The insights gained from this analysis are crucial for effective risk response planning and resource allocation, helping to ensure project success despite uncertainties.

EXECUTION OF RISK WEIGHTING AND CALCULATION OF RISK PRIORITY

Performing risk weighting and calculating risk priority are essential steps in quantitative risk analysis. This process involves assigning a relative weight or importance to each identified risk and then calculating its priority for management and mitigation. Here's a structured approach to perform this task:

1. Assigning Risk Weights

- **Criteria for Weighting**: Establish criteria for weighting risks, which could include factors like impact on project objectives, likelihood of occurrence, or stakeholder concerns.

- **Weighting Scale**: Use a numerical scale (e.g., 1 to 5 or 1 to 10) to assign weights to each risk. Higher numbers indicate higher importance or severity.

2. Calculating Risk Scores

- **Risk Score Formula**: Calculate the risk score for each risk, typically by multiplying the probability (likelihood) of each risk by its impact and weight. $RiskScore = Probability \times Impact \times Weight$

- **Quantitative Measures**: Where possible, use quantitative measures for probability and impact to increase the accuracy of the risk scores.

3. Prioritizing Risks Based on Scores

- **Ranking Risks**: Rank risks based on their calculated scores. Higher scores indicate higher priority risks that need more immediate attention and resources.

- **Risk Matrix**: Utilize a risk matrix to visually map and prioritize risks based on their scores.

4. Considering Other Factors

- **Stakeholder Input**: Consider stakeholder input and concerns as part of the prioritization process. Some risks may be more critical to stakeholders despite having a lower quantitative score.

- **External Factors**: Account for external factors such as regulatory changes or market conditions that might influence risk priority.

5. Documenting and Communicating Priorities

- **Risk Register Update**: Document the weighted scores and priorities of each risk in the risk register.

- **Clarity in Documentation**: Ensure that the methodology and rationale for weighting and prioritizing risks are clearly documented and transparent.

6. Review and Adjust Regularly

- **Dynamic Process**: Recognize that risk prioritization is a dynamic process. Regularly review and adjust risk weights and priorities as project conditions and external environments change.

- **Feedback Loop**: Implement a feedback loop where new information can be integrated into the risk prioritization process.

7. Incorporate into Risk Management Planning

- **Inform Risk Responses**: Use the prioritization to inform risk response strategies. Focus more resources and planning efforts on managing higher-priority risks.

- **Resource Allocation**: Ensure resource allocation aligns with the prioritization, dedicating more resources to higher-scored risks.

Conclusion

Risk weighting and calculating risk priority are critical for effective risk management. They provide a structured approach to evaluate and prioritize risks, enabling project managers to focus on the most significant risks. Regular reviews, stakeholder engagement, and adaptation to changing circumstances are key components of this process, ensuring that the risk management efforts are aligned with the project's current needs and objectives.

CASE STUDY: LARGE-SCALE SOFTWARE DEVELOPMENT PROJECT

Context

A technology company is undertaking a large-scale software development project to create a new customer relationship management (CRM) system. Given the complexity and importance of the project, performing a quantitative risk analysis is essential to understand and manage the risks effectively.

Analyzing Risk Data Against Established Metrics

- **Risk Metrics:** Utilizing metrics such as cost variance, schedule variance, defect rates, and delivery timelines.

- **Process Performance Review:** Comparing current project performance data against these metrics to identify areas of risk.

Analyzing General Risks of the Project

- **General Risk Assessment:** Identifying risks related to project management, technology, stakeholder engagement, and external factors like market trends.

- **Data-Driven Analysis:** Using historical and current project data to quantify the probability and impact of these general risks.

Performing Forecast and Trend Analysis

- **Historical Data Review:** Analyzing past projects' data to identify trends and patterns that might apply to the current project.

- **Forecasting:** Using statistical methods to forecast potential outcomes based on these trends and the current project data.

Performing Sensitivity Analysis

- **Monte Carlo Simulations:** Running simulations to understand the range of possible outcomes and their probabilities.

- **Decision Trees:** Using decision trees to analyze the implications of different decisions and their associated risks.

- **Critical Path Analysis:** Identifying and analyzing the risks associated with the critical path of the project schedule.

- **Expected Monetary Value Analysis:** Calculating the expected monetary value of risks to prioritize them based on their financial impact.

Performing Risk Weighting and Calculating Risk Priority

- **Risk Weighting:** Assigning weights to risks based on their impact and probability, considering factors such as project objectives and stakeholder concerns.

- **Risk Priority Calculation:** Using the weighted risks to calculate a risk priority score, which helps in prioritizing the risks for response planning.

Conclusion

In the context of the software development project, performing quantitative risk analysis involves a comprehensive approach to evaluating risk data against established metrics, analyzing general project risks, and conducting forecast and trend analyses. Sensitivity analysis, including Monte Carlo simulations, decision trees, and critical path analysis, provides a deeper understanding of the potential impact of risks. Risk weighting and priority calculations enable the project team to focus on the most significant risks. This quantitative approach complements qualitative analysis and aligns with PMI standards for risk management, ensuring that the project is well-positioned to manage risks effectively and achieve its objectives.

Task 3 Identify threats and opportunities

ASSESSMENT OF PROJECT RISK COMPLEXITY USING ANALYTICAL TOOLS

Assessing project risk complexity is a crucial task in identifying threats and opportunities. Techniques like SWOT analysis, Ishikawa diagrams, and Tree Diagrams can be effectively used to evaluate the intricacies of project risks. Here's how these methods can be applied:

1. SWOT Analysis

- **Methodology**: SWOT (Strengths, Weaknesses, Opportunities, Threats) analysis is a strategic planning tool used to evaluate the internal and external factors affecting a project.

- Application:

- **Strengths and Weaknesses**: Assess internal factors such as team capabilities, resources, and processes.

- **Opportunities and Threats**: Evaluate external factors like market trends, competition, and regulatory changes.

- **Risk Complexity Assessment**: Use SWOT to identify how internal and external factors contribute to the project's risk complexity.

2. Ishikawa (Cause and Effect) Diagrams

- **Methodology**: Ishikawa diagrams, also known as fishbone diagrams, are used to identify and represent the causes of a specific risk or problem.

- Application:

- **Identify Main Causes**: Break down risks into categories such as methods, materials, manpower, and machinery.

- **Sub-Causes**: Under each category, list specific factors that might contribute to the risk.

- **Risk Complexity Assessment**: Analyze how various factors interconnect and contribute to the overall risk landscape of the project.

3. Tree Diagrams

- **Methodology**: Tree diagrams are used to break down broad categories into finer levels of detail, showing the hierarchy of factors contributing to a risk.

- Application:

- **Structure the Risk**: Start with a broad risk category and break it down into specific, actionable elements.

- **Hierarchy of Risks**: Develop a hierarchical view of how each sub-risk relates to the main risk category.

- **Risk Complexity Assessment**: Use the tree diagram to visualize the complexity of risks and how different elements are interrelated.

Integrating These Methods

- **Complementary Use**: Each of these methods provides a unique perspective on risk complexity. They can be used in combination to gain a comprehensive understanding.

- **Stakeholder Involvement**: Engage project stakeholders in each of these exercises to gather diverse insights and perspectives.

Documenting and Communicating the Findings

- **Risk Register**: Document the findings from SWOT analysis, Ishikawa diagrams, and Tree diagrams in the risk register.

- **Reporting**: Create reports or presentations to communicate the outcomes of these analyses to stakeholders and decision-makers.

Conclusion

Assessing project risk complexity through methods like SWOT analysis, Ishikawa diagrams, and Tree diagrams helps in identifying and understanding the multifaceted nature of project risks. This comprehensive assessment is essential for developing effective risk management strategies and for facilitating stakeholder understanding and engagement in the risk management process.

IMPACT ANALYSIS ON PROJECT OBJECTIVES COVERING KEY PROJECT DIMENSIONS

Performing an impact analysis on project objectives involves assessing how potential risks could affect key areas of the project such as scope, schedule, cost, resources, quality, and stakeholders. This analysis helps in understanding the severity of risks and aids in prioritizing and developing risk response strategies. Here's a structured approach to conducting an impact analysis:

1. Impact on Project Scope

- **Assess Scope Changes**: Evaluate how identified risks could cause changes in project scope, including additions or reductions in project deliverables.

- **Consider Scope Creep**: Be aware of risks that could lead to scope creep, where uncontrolled changes or continuous growth in project scope occur without corresponding adjustments in time, cost, and resources.

2. Impact on Project Schedule

- **Schedule Delays or Accelerations**: Determine how risks might delay project milestones or, conversely, require an acceleration of the schedule.

- **Critical Path Analysis**: Use critical path analysis to identify which risks impact the critical tasks and milestones.

3. Impact on Project Cost

- **Cost Overruns or Savings**: Assess the potential for risks to increase costs (through delays, resource overuse, etc.) or potentially lead to cost savings (through efficiencies, cheaper alternatives, etc.).

- **Budget Contingency**: Consider the impact on the project's contingency budget and overall financial resources.

4. Impact on Resources

- **Resource Availability and Allocation**: Evaluate how risks might affect the availability and allocation of resources, including personnel, equipment, and materials.

- **Resource Overutilization or Underutilization**: Assess the risk of resource overutilization, which can lead to burnout or increased costs, or underutilization, which can lead to inefficiencies.

5. Impact on Quality

- **Quality Standards**: Examine how risks could impact the project's ability to meet established quality standards.

- **Quality Control Measures**: Consider the effect on quality control measures and the potential need for additional quality assurance processes.

6. Impact on Stakeholders

- **Stakeholder Expectations and Satisfaction**: Analyze how risks might affect stakeholder satisfaction, including clients, team members, and external parties.

- **Communication and Engagement**: Assess the impact on stakeholder communication and engagement, particularly if risks could lead to significant changes in project objectives or deliverables.

7. Documenting and Reporting the Analysis

- **Detailed Documentation**: Document the findings of the impact analysis in the risk register or a separate analysis report.

- **Visual Tools**: Use charts, graphs, and matrices to visually represent the impact of risks on different project objectives.

8. Review and Update Regularly

- **Dynamic Analysis**: Regularly update the impact analysis to reflect new risks and changes in the project environment.

- **Stakeholder Review**: Engage stakeholders in reviewing the impact analysis to ensure it remains relevant and accurate.

Conclusion

Conducting an impact analysis on project objectives is crucial in risk management, as it provides a clear understanding of how risks could affect various aspects of the project. This analysis forms the basis for prioritizing risks and developing effective mitigation strategies, ensuring that the project remains aligned with its goals despite potential uncertainties.

ALIGNMENT ASSESSMENT OF PROJECT COMPLIANCE OBJECTIVES WITH ORGANIZATIONAL STRATEGIC GOALS

Assessing project compliance objectives against organizational strategic objectives is a critical exercise in ensuring that a project aligns with the broader goals and governance standards of the organization. This assessment includes evaluating how well the project adheres to established procedures, project plans, corporate and project governance policies, as well as regulatory requirements. Here's a structured approach to conducting this assessment:

1. Understand Organizational Strategic Objectives

- **Review Organizational Goals**: Start by thoroughly understanding the strategic objectives of the organization. This includes long-term goals, mission, vision, and values.

- **Alignment with Strategy**: Assess how the project's objectives align with these broader strategic goals. Ensure the project contributes positively to the overall direction of the organization.

2. Evaluate Compliance with Procedures and Project Plans

- **Standard Procedures**: Review the project's adherence to standard operating procedures established by the organization. This can include processes for quality control, financial reporting, and communication.

- **Adherence to Project Plans**: Assess whether the project is following its defined plans, including scope, schedule, and budget compliance.

3. Assess Corporate and Project Governance Compliance

- **Governance Policies**: Evaluate the project's compliance with corporate governance policies. This includes management structures, decision making processes, and accountability mechanisms.

- **Project Governance**: Specifically assess the project's own governance structure. Ensure that it meets the standards for effective project oversight, risk management, and stakeholder engagement.

4. Review Regulatory and Legal Compliance

- **Regulatory Standards**: Check compliance with relevant industry regulations and legal requirements. This may involve environmental regulations, health and safety standards, labor laws, and financial regulations.

- **Documentation and Reporting**: Ensure that all necessary regulatory documentation and reporting are being accurately maintained and submitted.

5. Document the Assessment

- **Compliance Report**: Create a detailed compliance report outlining how the project aligns with organizational objectives and complies with relevant procedures and regulations.

- **Identify Gaps and Recommendations**: In the report, highlight any areas of non-compliance or misalignment with strategic objectives, along with recommendations for improvement.

6. Engage Stakeholders

- **Stakeholder Review**: Present the findings to key project stakeholders, including project sponsors, senior management, and project team members.

- **Feedback Incorporation**: Use feedback from these stakeholders to refine the assessment and address any concerns.

7. Implement Improvement Actions

- **Action Plan**: Develop an action plan to address any areas of non-compliance or misalignment.

- **Monitor Progress**: Regularly monitor the project's progress in implementing these improvements and maintaining compliance.

Conclusion

Assessing a project's compliance with organizational strategic objectives is key to ensuring that the project not only meets its immediate goals but also contributes to the broader aims of the organization. This comprehensive assessment involves a thorough review of adherence to procedures, governance standards, and regulatory requirements, and necessitates engagement with key stakeholders to ensure alignment and address any discrepancies. Regular monitoring and adaptation are essential for maintaining this alignment throughout the project lifecycle.

EMPOWERING STAKEHOLDERS FOR INDEPENDENT IDENTIFICATION OF THREATS AND OPPORTUNITIES

Empowering stakeholders to independently identify threats and opportunities is a crucial aspect of participatory risk management. It involves enabling and encouraging stakeholders to actively engage in the risk identification process. This approach leads to a more comprehensive and diverse understanding of potential risks and opportunities. Here's a guide on how to empower stakeholders:

1. Educate and Train Stakeholders

- **Risk Management Training**: Provide training sessions for stakeholders on the basics of risk management, including how to identify and assess risks.

- **Tools and Techniques**: Teach them about various tools and techniques for identifying risks, such as brainstorming sessions, SWOT analysis (Strengths, Weaknesses, Opportunities, Threats), and PESTLE analysis (Political, Economic, Social, Technological, Legal, and Environmental).

2. Provide Necessary Tools and Resources

- **Access to Information**: Ensure stakeholders have access to all necessary project information and data to identify risks accurately.

- **Risk Identification Templates**: Provide templates or checklists that stakeholders can use to record identified risks.

3. Create an Open Communication Environment

- **Encourage Sharing**: Foster an environment where stakeholders feel comfortable sharing their observations and concerns.

- **Regular Meetings**: Hold regular meetings where stakeholders can discuss potential risks and opportunities.

4. Involve Stakeholders in Decision-Making

- **Inclusive Discussions**: Include stakeholders in risk management discussions and decision-making processes.

- **Valuing Input**: Acknowledge the importance of their contributions and demonstrate how their input is being used in the project.

5. Feedback Mechanisms

- **Establish Feedback Channels**: Set up clear channels through which stakeholders can report identified risks, such as dedicated email addresses, online platforms, or regular meetings.

- **Act on Feedback**: Ensure that there is a process in place to evaluate and act upon the risks identified by stakeholders.

6. Encourage a Proactive Approach

- **Promote Risk Awareness**: Encourage stakeholders to be proactive in identifying risks and opportunities, rather than waiting for issues to emerge.

- **Reward Initiative**: Recognize and reward stakeholders who actively participate in the risk identification process.

7. Regular Reviews and Updates

- **Update Risk Management Plan**: Regularly review and update the risk management plan to incorporate new risks and opportunities identified by stakeholders.

- **Continuous Improvement**: Use stakeholder feedback to continuously improve the risk identification process.

Conclusion

Empowering stakeholders to independently identify threats and opportunities enhances the risk management process by leveraging diverse perspectives and expertise. It requires providing adequate training, tools, and an open communication environment. Regular engagement, feedback mechanisms, and acknowledging stakeholders' contributions are key to maintaining an active and effective stakeholder participation in risk management.

CASE STUDY: INTERNATIONAL MANUFACTURING FACILITY EXPANSION

Context

A multinational manufacturing company is planning to expand its facilities into new international markets. This expansion project is complex, involving various risks and opportunities that must be identified and managed effectively.

Assessing Project Risk Complexity

- **SWOT Analysis:** Conducting a Strengths, Weaknesses, Opportunities, and Threats analysis to understand internal capabilities and external market conditions.

- **Ishikawa (Cause-and-Effect) Diagram:** Using Ishikawa diagrams to trace potential risks back to their root causes in areas like supply chain, technology, and human resources.

- **Tree Diagrams:** Utilizing tree diagrams to break down and categorize complex risks into more manageable components.

Performing an Impact Analysis on Project Objectives

- **Scope Impact:** Evaluating how identified risks could affect the scope of the facility expansion, such as changes in site requirements or design modifications.

- **Schedule and Cost Impact:** Assessing the potential for delays and cost overruns, considering factors like local regulations, labor availability, and material costs.

- **Resource Impact:** Analyzing the availability and reliability of resources, including workforce, technology, and capital.

- **Quality Impact:** Considering risks to the quality of construction and final outputs, aligned with the company's standards.

- **Stakeholder Impact:** Identifying how risks could affect various stakeholders, including local communities, employees, and shareholders.

Assessing Project Compliance Objectives Against Organizational Strategic Objectives

- **Alignment with Corporate Governance:** Ensuring the project adheres to the company's overall governance framework, including ethical standards and business practices.

- **Regulatory Governance Compliance:** Checking adherence to local and international regulatory requirements, particularly in new markets where regulations may differ significantly.

- **Project Plan Conformity:** Reviewing the project plans to ensure they align with the strategic objectives of the organization.

Empowering Stakeholders to Independently Identify Threats and Opportunities

- **Training and Workshops:** Organizing sessions to educate stakeholders on risk identification techniques and the specific context of the project

- **Feedback Mechanisms:** Establishing channels for stakeholders to report potential risks and opportunities they identify.

- **Inclusive Decision-Making:** Encouraging active participation from stakeholders in the risk management process to leverage diverse perspectives and insights.

Conclusion

In the international facility expansion project, identifying threats and opportunities involves a thorough assessment of project risk complexity using tools like SWOT analysis, Ishikawa diagrams, and tree diagrams. Impact analysis on project objectives, including scope, schedule, cost, resources, quality, and stakeholders, is crucial. Aligning project compliance with organizational strategic objectives ensures that the expansion aligns with broader company goals. Empowering stakeholders to identify risks and opportunities fosters a proactive risk management culture, essential in managing the complexities of an international expansion. This approach aligns with PMI standards for risk management, ensuring a comprehensive and inclusive strategy that enhances the project's chances of success in the global market.

DOMAIN IV
RISK RESPONSE

Task 1 Plan risk response

DETERMINATION OF APPROPRIATE RISK RESPONSE STRATEGIES

Determining the appropriate risk response strategy is a pivotal task in Domain IV Risk Response. This involves choosing the most effective way to address each identified risk, based on its nature, impact, and probability. The common risk response strategies include avoidance, acceptance, mitigation, enhancement, and contingency planning. Here's how to approach the selection of these strategies:

1. Avoidance

- **Applicability**: Used when a risk can be eliminated by changing project plans or approaches.

- **Strategy**: Alter aspects of the project to remove the risk entirely. This could involve changing suppliers, modifying project scope, altering timelines, or adopting different technologies.

- **Consideration**: Be aware that avoidance might sometimes lead to missing potential opportunities.

2. Acceptance

- **Applicability**: Applied when the impact of the risk is low or the cost of other strategies is not justified.

- **Strategy**: Accept the possibility of the risk occurring, without actively trying to change its probability or impact.

- **Passive and Active Acceptance**: Passive acceptance requires no action other than documenting the strategy, while active acceptance may involve establishing a contingency reserve or plan.

3. Mitigation

- **Applicability**: Suitable for risks with potentially significant impacts on the project.

- **Strategy**: Take proactive steps to reduce the probability of the risk occurring or lessen its impact if it does. This could include implementing additional quality controls, providing extra training, or conducting more thorough project planning.

- **Focus**: Aim to bring the risk to an acceptable threshold.

4. Enhancement

- **Applicability**: Applied to positive risks or opportunities.

- **Strategy**: Enhance the probability or the positive impacts of these opportunities. This could involve allocating more resources to an innovative part of the project to maximize its success.

- **Goal**: Increase the likelihood of realizing a positive risk or opportunity.

5. Contingency Planning

- **Applicability**: Used for risks that cannot be fully mitigated or avoided.

- **Strategy**: Develop plans to be implemented if the risk occurs. This includes identifying triggers and having resources or actions ready to deploy.

- **Preparation**: Ensure contingency plans are practical, time-bound, and clearly specify who is responsible for enacting them.

Conclusion

Selecting the appropriate risk response strategy requires a thorough understanding of each risk's characteristics and its potential impact on the project. The strategy should align with the project's overall objectives and resource availability. It's essential to document these strategies clearly and communicate them to all relevant stakeholders. Regular reviews and adjustments of the risk response strategies are also crucial, as project conditions and risk profiles can change over time.

DECISION-MAKING ON TIME-BOUND RISK RESPONSE ACTIONS AND IDENTIFICATION OF ACTION OWNERS

Deciding risk response actions that are time-bound and based on the chosen risk response strategies involves defining specific actions to manage each identified risk, setting timelines for these actions, and assigning responsible individuals or teams (action owners). Here's how to approach this:

1. Define Specific Risk Response Actions

- **Action Planning**: For each risk, develop specific actions that align with the chosen response strategy (avoid, accept, mitigate, enhance, contingency planning).

- **Detailing Actions**: Clearly outline what needs to be done, how it should be done, and the resources required.

2. Set Time Frames for Actions

- **Deadline Establishment**: Assign a deadline or time frame to each risk response action. This ensures that actions are carried out in a timely manner and helps in tracking progress.

- **Realistic Scheduling**: Ensure that the deadlines are realistic, considering the complexity of actions and available resources.

3. Assign Action Owners

- **Identify Responsible Individuals**: Assign an owner to each risk response action. This person or team will be responsible for ensuring the action is completed effectively.

- **Criteria for Assignment**: Choose owners based on their expertise, roles, authority, and availability.

4. Integrate Actions into Project Plans

- **Update Project Plans**: Incorporate the risk response actions into the overall project plan, including schedules, budgets, and resource allocations.

- **Alignment with Project Objectives**: Ensure that the actions align with and support the broader project objectives.

5. Document Actions and Owners

- **Risk Register Update**: Document each risk response action, its timeline, and the assigned owner in the risk register.

- **Action Plans**: Create detailed action plans or worksheets for complex actions, providing more in-depth guidance for action owners.

6. Communicate with Stakeholders

- **Clear Communication**: Communicate the risk response actions, timelines, and ownership to all relevant stakeholders, ensuring clarity and transparency.

- **Expectation Setting**: Set clear expectations with action owners regarding their responsibilities and the importance of meeting deadlines.

7. Monitor and Review Actions

- **Tracking Progress**: Regularly track the progress of risk response actions against their deadlines.

- **Adaptation and Adjustment**: Be prepared to adapt and adjust actions as needed based on their effectiveness and any changes in the project environment.

Conclusion

Deciding on time-bound risk response actions and assigning action owners is crucial for proactive risk management. This process requires careful planning, realistic scheduling, and clear communication. Regular monitoring and willingness to adapt actions as necessary are key to ensuring that risks are managed effectively throughout the lifecycle of the project.

EVALUATION OF RISK RESPONSE ACTIONS RELATIVE TO STRATEGY AND PROJECT OBJECTIVES

Assessing the effectiveness of risk response actions against the identified strategy and the impact on project objectives is a vital aspect of risk management. This assessment ensures that the actions taken are indeed mitigating risks effectively and contributing positively towards meeting project goals. Here's how to approach this assessment:

1. Review Risk Response Actions and Strategies

- **Action and Strategy Alignment**: Verify that the implemented risk response actions align with the initially identified strategies (avoid, accept, mitigate, enhance, or plan contingencies).

- **Initial Objectives**: Revisit the original objectives of each risk response action, focusing on the desired outcome in terms of reducing probability or impact.

2. Measure Impact on Project Objectives

- **Cost Impact**: Assess whether the risk response actions have led to cost savings, cost overruns, or have stayed neutral. Determine if these financial outcomes align with the project's budgetary objectives.

- **Schedule Impact**: Evaluate the effect of the risk responses on the project schedule. This includes any acceleration or delays resulting from the actions taken.

- **Quality and Scope Impact**: Review how the actions have influenced the project's quality and scope. Ensure that the responses have not inadvertently caused scope creep or quality degradation.

- **Environmental and Other Impacts**: Consider any additional impacts, like environmental or social, that may have been influenced by the risk responses.

3. Analyze Effectiveness in Risk Mitigation

- **Reduced Probability and Impact**: Analyze whether the risk responses have effectively reduced the likelihood of risks occurring and/or their potential impact.

- **Residual Risks**: Identify any residual risks that remain even after the response actions have been implemented.

4. Gather Feedback and Data

- **Stakeholder Feedback**: Collect feedback from the project team, stakeholders, and possibly clients to gain different perspectives on the effectiveness of the risk responses.

- **Quantitative Data**: Use quantitative metrics and data to support the assessment. This could include tracking changes in risk metrics pre- and post-implementation of the response actions.

5. Document the Findings

- **Update Risk Register**: Document the assessment results in the risk register, detailing the effectiveness of each risk response action.

- **Lessons Learned**: Capture lessons learned during the process, which can be used for future projects or ongoing project adjustments.

6. Communicate Results and Take Action

- **Reporting to Stakeholders**: Communicate the findings of the assessment to all relevant stakeholders, providing transparency about what is working and what is not.

- **Adjustment of Strategies**: Based on the assessment, adjust risk response strategies as needed to enhance their effectiveness or to address any uncovered issues.

Conclusion

Regularly assessing the effectiveness of risk response actions is essential to ensure that they are contributing positively to project objectives and effectively managing risks. This process involves a combination of quantitative analysis and qualitative feedback, leading to informed decisions about ongoing risk management strategies and actions.

ILLUSTRATION AND COMMUNICATION OF RISK RESPONSE STRATEGY EFFECTIVENESS

Illustrating and communicating the effectiveness of risk response strategies is crucial in risk management. Visual tools like risk burndown charts and dot plots can be very effective in this regard. These tools provide a clear, understandable way to convey complex information to stakeholders. Here's how to use these tools:

1. Risk Burndown Chart

- **Purpose**: A risk burndown chart shows the reduction of risk over time as response strategies are implemented.

- How to Create:

- **Vertical Axis**: Represent the total risk exposure, which could be a composite measure of all risks based on their probability and impact.

- **Horizontal Axis**: Show the timeline of the project.

- **Plotting Risk Exposure**: At regular intervals (e.g., weekly, monthly), plot the current total risk exposure. This will typically reduce over time as risks are mitigated.

- **Interpretation**: The downward slope of the chart indicates the reduction of risk. Plateaus or increases in the line might indicate new risks or ineffective risk responses.

2. Dot Plots

- **Purpose**: Dot plots are used to show the distribution and status of risks at a point in time.

- How to Create:

- **Axes**: Use one axis for the probability of risks and the other for their impact.

- **Plotting Risks**: Place a dot for each risk based on its probability and impact. You can use different colors or sizes of dots to represent different categories of risks or changes over time.

- **Interpretation**: Dot plots provide a snapshot of risk status, helping stakeholders quickly understand which risks are most critical.

3. Communicating Using These Tools

- **Regular Updates**: Update these visualizations regularly and include them in project status reports or risk management updates.

- **Stakeholder Meetings**: Present these charts in stakeholder meetings to facilitate discussions about risk management progress and effectiveness.

- **Clear Explanations**: When presenting these tools, clearly explain what they represent and how to interpret them. Not all stakeholders may be familiar with these types of visual data representations.

4. Incorporating Feedback

- **Feedback Mechanism**: Encourage stakeholders to provide feedback on the risk management process and the usefulness of the visual tools in understanding risk response effectiveness.

- **Adjustments Based on Feedback**: Be prepared to adjust your communication strategy or the visual tools based on this feedback to ensure clarity and effectiveness.

Conclusion

Visual tools like risk burndown charts and dot plots are effective means for illustrating and communicating the effectiveness of risk response strategies. They provide a clear, concise way to convey complex risk management information, making it easier for stakeholders to understand and engage with the risk management process. Regular updates, clear explanations, and stakeholder feedback are key to ensuring these tools are as effective as possible.

DETERMINING EFFECTIVE WORKAROUNDS FOR UNFORESEEN RISKS

Determining a workaround in project risk management involves creating a temporary solution to deal with an unforeseen problem or risk that cannot be managed by the original plan. Workarounds are typically used to address issues that are unexpected or have not been previously identified in the risk management plan. Here's how to approach this:

1. Identify the Need for a Workaround

- **Unexpected Issues**: Recognize situations where existing risk plans are insufficient, and an immediate, unplanned response is necessary.

- **Assess Urgency**: Determine the urgency of the issue to decide how quickly a workaround needs to be implemented.

2. Analyze the Problem

- **Understand the Issue**: Thoroughly analyze the problem to understand its nature, scope, and potential impact on the project.

- **Root Cause Analysis**: Conduct a root cause analysis to understand why the issue occurred, which can inform the development of an effective workaround.

3. Develop Workaround Options

- **Brainstorming Solutions**: Engage the project team in brainstorming potential temporary solutions to the problem.

- **Feasibility and Impact Assessment**: Assess the feasibility of each proposed workaround and its potential impact on the project, including any new risks that might be introduced.

4. Select the Most Appropriate Workaround

- **Criteria for Selection**: Choose a workaround based on criteria such as ease of implementation, cost, time, resource availability, and least disruption to the project.

- **Stakeholder Input**: Involve key stakeholders in the decision-making process to ensure the workaround aligns with project objectives and stakeholder expectations.

5. Implement the Workaround

- **Action Plan**: Develop a clear action plan for implementing the workaround, including steps, resources needed, and responsibilities.

- **Communication**: Communicate the plan to the project team and stakeholders, ensuring everyone understands their roles and the reasons for the workaround.

6. Monitor and Review the Workaround

- **Track Effectiveness**: Closely monitor the implementation of the workaround to ensure it is effectively addressing the issue.

- **Adjust as Needed**: Be prepared to adjust the workaround if it is not working as expected or if new issues arise.

7. Document the Process

- **Record Keeping**: Document the problem, the analysis process, the rationale for choosing the workaround, and the implementation plan.

- **Lessons Learned**: Capture lessons learned from the experience to improve future risk management practices.

8. Plan for Long-Term Resolution

- **Transition Plan**: Develop a plan to transition from the workaround to a permanent solution, if applicable.

- **Update Risk Management Plan**: Revise the project's risk management plan to include the newly identified risk and the corresponding long-term response strategies.

Alexander Stratton

Conclusion

Workarounds are essential for addressing unforeseen problems that arise during a project. They require quick thinking, thorough analysis, and effective team communication. While workarounds provide a temporary solution, it's important to also plan for a long-term resolution and update the risk management plan accordingly to accommodate new learnings and strategies.

ALLOCATION OF RESPONSIBILITIES IN RISK MANAGEMENT

Allocating responsibilities in risk management is a crucial step in ensuring that each identified risk is effectively managed. This involves assigning specific risk-related tasks to appropriate team members or stakeholders based on their skills, experience, and roles within the project. Here's a structured approach to allocating responsibilities:

1. Identify Risk-Related Tasks

- **Break Down Actions**: For each identified risk and its corresponding response strategy, break down the required actions into specific tasks.

- **Detail Requirements**: Define what each task entails, including its scope, objectives, and any necessary resources.

2. Assess Team Skills and Availability

- **Skill Assessment**: Evaluate the skills, experience, and expertise of project team members and other stakeholders.

- **Availability Check**: Consider the current workload and availability of potential assignees to ensure they have the capacity to take on the responsibility.

3. Match Tasks with Team Members

- **Responsibility Assignment**: Match each task with the most suitable team member or stakeholder. Assign tasks based on individuals' strengths and areas of expertise.

- **Diverse Skills Utilization**: Utilize the diverse skills within the team to cover different types of risk effectively.

4. Define Roles and Expectations

- **Clear Definitions**: Clearly define the role and expectations for each individual regarding their risk-related responsibilities.

- **Responsibility Matrix**: Use a Responsibility Assignment Matrix (RAM), such as a RACI chart (Responsible, Accountable, Consulted, Informed), to delineate responsibilities and roles.

5. Communicate Allocations

- **Inform Team Members**: Communicate the responsibility allocations to all team members, ensuring everyone understands their roles and the importance of their tasks.

- **Stakeholder Communication**: Inform stakeholders of who is responsible for managing key risks, especially if stakeholder involvement or support is needed.

6. Provide Necessary Support and Resources

- **Resource Allocation**: Ensure that each responsible individual has access to the necessary resources to perform their tasks effectively.

- **Training and Support**: Provide training or support where needed, especially if the task involves handling complex or high-impact risks.

7. Monitor and Review

- **Ongoing Oversight**: Regularly monitor the progress of risk management tasks and the performance of individuals responsible for these tasks.

- **Adapt and Adjust**: Be prepared to reallocate responsibilities or provide additional support if challenges arise or if the project environment changes.

Conclusion

Effective allocation of responsibilities in risk management is key to ensuring that risks are managed proactively and efficiently. It requires a clear understanding of team capabilities, careful matching of tasks with individuals, and ongoing monitoring and support. Clear communication and a well-defined responsibility matrix are essential to maintain clarity and accountability throughout the project.

DEVELOPMENT OF A RESPONSIBILITY MATRIX IN A METRICIZED PROJECT ENVIRONMENT

Outlining an appropriate responsibility matrix in a metricized project environment involves defining specific roles and responsibilities for project tasks, particularly those related to risk management, and aligning them with key performance indicators (KPIs) and metrics. A common tool used for this purpose is the RACI matrix (Responsible, Accountable, Consulted, Informed). Here's how to create a RACI matrix in a metricized project environment:

1. Identify Key Tasks and Metrics

- **List Tasks**: Start by listing all major tasks and activities related to risk management in the project, such as risk identification, analysis, response planning, and monitoring.

- **Define Metrics**: For each task, define relevant metrics or KPIs that will be used to measure success or progress. This could include metrics like risk reduction percentage, number of risks identified, or adherence to risk response timelines.

2. Define RACI Categories

- **Responsible (R)**: Individuals or teams who will perform the task.

- **Accountable (A)**: The person ultimately accountable for the task's completion and quality. This person approves work and is the final decision-maker. Typically, this is one individual.

- **Consulted (C)**: Those who provide input based on their expertise. Their opinions are sought, and they have a two-way communication.

- **Informed (I)**: Those who need to be kept up-to-date on progress or decisions. They have a one-way communication.

3. Assign Roles for Each Task

- **Distribute Roles**: For each task, assign team members or stakeholders to the RACI categories. Ensure that each task has at least one person Responsible and one Accountable.

- **Alignment with Metrics**: Ensure that the individuals assigned to Responsible and Accountable roles are capable of influencing the respective metrics for each task.

4. Integrate Metric Tracking

- **Metric Ownership**: Assign ownership of each metric to the most relevant person or role, typically the one Accountable. This individual will ensure that metrics are tracked and targets are met.

- **Reporting Structure**: Define how and when metrics will be reported and reviewed.

5. Communicate the Matrix

- **Share with Team**: Share the RACI matrix with your project team and stakeholders. Ensure everyone understands their roles and the importance of the associated metrics.

- **Feedback Loop**: Allow for feedback and make adjustments as needed to ensure clarity and practicality.

6. Review and Update Regularly

- **Regular Reviews**: Regularly review the RACI matrix and the effectiveness of the metric tracking to ensure alignment with project objectives and changes in the project environment.

- **Adapt as Needed**: Be prepared to make adjustments to the matrix as the project progresses or if roles change.

Conclusion

A RACI matrix in a metricized project environment helps to clarify roles and responsibilities in risk management and ensures that each task is aligned with specific metrics. This clear delineation of duties, combined with a focus on measurable outcomes, is crucial for effective project and risk management. Regular communication, review, and adjustment of the matrix are key to maintaining its relevance and effectiveness throughout the project.

REASSESSMENT OF ORGANIZATIONAL RISKS

Re-evaluating organizational risks is a continuous and critical process in risk management, particularly as internal and external environments evolve. This involves periodically reviewing and updating the organization's risk profile to ensure that new risks are identified, and existing risks are still relevant and appropriately managed. Here's a structured approach to re-evaluating organizational risks:

Alexander Stratton

1. Review Current Risk Environment

- **Existing Risk Register**: Start by reviewing the current risk register to assess the status of known risks.

- **Environmental Changes**: Evaluate changes in the external and internal environments that could affect the risk landscape, such as market shifts, technological advancements, regulatory changes, or internal operational adjustments.

2. Identify New Risks

- **Brainstorming Sessions**: Conduct brainstorming sessions with key stakeholders to identify new risks that have emerged since the last evaluation.

- **Industry Analysis**: Analyze industry trends and benchmark against peer organizations to uncover risks that may not have been previously considered.

3. Assess and Update Risk Impact and Probability

- **Reassess Existing Risks**: Re-evaluate the impact and probability of existing risks. Determine if these assessments need to be adjusted due to changing conditions.

- **Rank New Risks**: Assess the impact and probability of new risks and rank them accordingly.

4. Update Risk Response Strategies

- **Review Strategies**: Review existing risk response strategies to ensure they are still effective and relevant.

- **Adjust Strategies**: Adjust or develop new strategies for mitigating, transferring, avoiding, or accepting risks based on the updated risk profile.

5. Engage with Stakeholders

- **Stakeholder Consultation**: Engage with various stakeholders, including department heads, project managers, and external experts, for a comprehensive view of risks.

- **Feedback Incorporation**: Incorporate feedback from these stakeholders into the risk re-evaluation process.

6. Monitor Leading Risk Indicators

- **Identify Indicators**: Identify leading indicators that can provide early warnings of risk materialization.

- **Continuous Monitoring**: Set up a system for continuous monitoring of these indicators.

7. Document and Communicate Changes

- **Updated Documentation**: Update the risk management documentation, including the risk register, to reflect the re-evaluated risks and strategies.

- **Clear Communication**: Communicate changes in the risk profile and response strategies to all relevant stakeholders, ensuring clarity and alignment.

8. Plan for Regular Reviews

- **Scheduled Reviews**: Establish a regular schedule for re-evaluating organizational risks, considering the dynamic nature of business operations and external environments.

- **Adaptive Approach**: Be prepared to conduct unscheduled reviews in response to significant internal changes or external events.

Conclusion

Re-evaluating organizational risks is an ongoing process that adapts to changes in both the internal and external environment. It ensures that the organization's risk management strategies are current, effective, and aligned with its overall objectives. This process requires a comprehensive approach, involving continuous monitoring, stakeholder engagement, and the flexibility to adjust strategies as needed.

CASE STUDY: CROSS-COUNTRY OIL PIPELINE CONSTRUCTION

Context

An energy company is undertaking a cross-country oil pipeline construction project. This high-stakes project faces various risks, from environmental concerns to technical challenges and regulatory compliance. Planning an effective risk response is crucial to manage these risks successfully.

Determining Appropriate Risk Response Strategy

- **Avoidance:** Changing project plans to eliminate certain risks, such as rerouting the pipeline to avoid environmentally sensitive areas.

- **Acceptance:** Acknowledging certain unavoidable risks, like regulatory changes, and preparing to manage their impact.

- **Mitigation:** Implementing measures to reduce the likelihood or impact of risks, such as employing advanced safety protocols to minimize accident risks.

- **Enhancement:** Identifying and leveraging opportunities to enhance project outcomes, like using state-of-the-art technology to increase efficiency.

- **Contingency Planning:** Developing plans for potential scenarios, like supply chain disruptions.

Deciding Risk Response Actions

- **Action Plans:** Outlining specific, time-bound actions for each risk response strategy.

- **Action Owners:** Assigning responsibility for each action to specific team members or departments.

Assessing Effectiveness of Risk Response Actions

- **Effectiveness Against Strategy:** Evaluating how well the actions align with the chosen risk response strategies.

- **Impact on Project Objectives:** Assessing the effect of the actions on project costs, schedule, and environmental impact.

- **Probability and Impact Adjustment:** Analyzing how the actions have changed the probability or impact of the risks.

Illustrating and Communicating Effectiveness

- **Risk Burndown Chart:** Using a burndown chart to visually represent the reduction of risk over time.

- **Dot Plots:** Employing dot plots to illustrate the status of various risks and the effectiveness of response actions.

Determining Workarounds

- **Identifying Workarounds:** Developing immediate, short-term solutions for risks that materialize unexpectedly.

Allocating Responsibilities

- **Clear Assignment:** Ensuring all risk response actions have clearly designated responsible parties.

Outlining a Responsibility Matrix

- **RACI Chart:** Creating a Responsibility, Accountability, Consultation, and Information (RACI) chart to clarify roles and responsibilities in a metricized project environment.

Re-evaluating Organizational Risks

- **Continuous Assessment:** Regularly reviewing and updating the risk assessment to reflect changes in the project environment and organization.

Conclusion

For the cross-country oil pipeline construction project, planning risk responses involves determining appropriate strategies, assigning actions and owners, and assessing the effectiveness of these actions. By utilizing tools like risk burndown charts and RACI charts, the project risk manager can effectively communicate and manage the risk response process. The approach not only aligns with PMI standards for risk management but also ensures that the project adapts to changing conditions and maintains alignment with organizational objectives. Through this comprehensive risk response planning, the project is better positioned to navigate the complexities and uncertainties inherent in such a large-scale infrastructure project.

Task 2 Implement risk response

IMPLEMENTATION OF RISK RESPONSE PLANS

Executing the risk response plans is a critical phase in project risk management, where the planned strategies for managing identified risks are put into action. Effective execution requires coordination, communication, and adaptability. Here's how to approach this task:

1. Initiate Risk Response Actions

- **Activate Plans**: Begin by activating the risk response actions as outlined in the risk management plan. This includes both proactive strategies for anticipated risks and reactive measures for emerging risks.

- **Resource Allocation**: Ensure that the necessary resources (people, budget, equipment) are allocated and available for executing the risk response actions.

2. Coordinate with Relevant Stakeholders

- **Communication**: Clearly communicate the risk response plans to all involved stakeholders, including what actions are to be taken, by whom, and when.

- **Roles and Responsibilities**: Confirm that everyone understands their roles and responsibilities in the execution of the plan.

3. Monitor and Supervise Execution

- **Oversight**: Provide oversight and support to the individuals or teams responsible for executing each risk response action.

- **Tracking Progress**: Use project management tools or systems to track the progress of risk response actions against timelines and milestones.

4. Ensure Alignment with Project Objectives

- **Consistency Check**: Regularly check that the risk response actions are aligned with the overall project objectives and goals. Ensure that the actions taken are not inadvertently impacting the project negatively.

5. Adapt and Adjust Risk Responses

- **Flexibility**: Be prepared to adapt and adjust risk responses as needed based on their effectiveness and any changes in project circumstances or risk status.

- **Problem-Solving**: Address any issues or challenges that arise during the execution of the risk response plans promptly and effectively.

6. Documentation and Reporting

- **Record-Keeping**: Maintain detailed records of the execution of risk response actions, including dates of action, persons involved, and outcomes.

- **Regular Reporting**: Provide regular updates to project stakeholders on the status and effectiveness of the risk response actions.

7. Leverage Technology and Tools

- **Project Management Software**: Utilize project management software tools to facilitate the coordination, tracking, and reporting of risk response activities.

- **Collaboration Tools**: Use collaboration tools to enhance communication and coordination among team members and stakeholders.

Conclusion

Executing risk response plans effectively is essential for mitigating risks and ensuring project success. It involves careful planning, clear communication, active monitoring, and the flexibility to adapt as the project progresses. Maintaining alignment with overall project objectives and thorough documentation are key aspects of successful execution. Regular stakeholder engagement and feedback are also vital to ensure the risk responses are appropriate and effective.

ACTIVATION AND IMPLEMENTATION OF CONTINGENCY PLANS

Executing contingency plans in project risk management involves implementing specific actions designed for scenarios where identified risks materialize. Contingency plans are essentially "backup plans" activated when certain triggers or conditions are met. Here's a structured approach to executing these plans:

1. Identify Contingency Plan Activation Triggers

- **Define Triggers**: Clearly define the specific conditions or triggers that will prompt the activation of a contingency plan. These could be events, indicators, or thresholds that signal a risk has materialized.

- **Awareness Among Team**: Ensure that all project team members and relevant stakeholders are aware of these triggers.

2. Activate Contingency Plans

- **Trigger Occurrence**: Once a trigger event occurs, promptly activate the relevant contingency plan. Timely activation is key to effectively managing the risk.

- **Communication**: Communicate the activation of the contingency plan to all relevant stakeholders, outlining the next steps and expected actions.

3. Implement Contingency Actions

- **Follow Planned Steps**: Execute the steps outlined in the contingency plan. This may involve reallocating resources, adjusting project schedules, or implementing alternative processes.

- **Coordination**: Ensure coordinated efforts among different team members and departments involved in executing the plan.

4. Monitor and Supervise Implementation

- **Ongoing Oversight**: Provide continuous oversight and support during the implementation of the contingency plan.

- **Track Progress**: Use project management tools to monitor the progress and effectiveness of the contingency actions.

5. Assess Impact on Project

- **Evaluate Impact**: Regularly assess the impact of the contingency plan's implementation on the overall project objectives, schedule, budget, and quality.

- **Adjust Project Plan**: Make necessary adjustments to the project plan to account for the changes brought by implementing the contingency plan.

6. Document and Report Execution

- **Record-Keeping**: Maintain detailed records of the execution of the contingency plan, including what actions were taken, by whom, and when.

- **Reporting**: Provide regular updates to project stakeholders on the status of the contingency plan implementation and its impact on the project.

7. Feedback and Adjustment

- **Gather Feedback**: Obtain feedback from team members and stakeholders on the effectiveness of the contingency plan.

- **Continuous Improvement**: Use the feedback and lessons learned to refine the contingency plan and improve future risk response strategies.

Conclusion

Executing contingency plans is a critical component of effective risk management. It requires clear triggers, prompt activation, coordinated execution, and ongoing monitoring and adjustment. Transparent communication, meticulous documentation, and stakeholder engagement are essential throughout the process to ensure that the contingency actions align with the overall project objectives and adapt to evolving project needs.

FACILITATION OF STAKEHOLDER FEEDBACK ON RISK RESPONSE MEASURES

Encouraging stakeholders to provide feedback on the risk response is an essential part of effective risk management. It ensures that the risk response strategies are working as intended and allows for continuous improvement. Here's a structured approach to facilitate this feedback:

1. Communicate the Importance of Feedback

- **Explain Benefits**: Clearly articulate to stakeholders the importance of their feedback in refining risk responses and enhancing project outcomes.

- **Inclusive Approach**: Emphasize that risk management is a collaborative process and that stakeholder insights are valuable in making informed decisions.

2. Provide Easy Channels for Feedback

- **Accessible Platforms**: Set up easily accessible channels for stakeholders to provide their feedback. This could include surveys, feedback forms, email, or dedicated sessions in meetings.

- **Regular Surveys**: Conduct regular surveys focused on specific aspects of the risk response strategies.

3. Engage Proactively with Stakeholders

- **Regular Meetings**: Organize regular meetings or workshops with stakeholders where they can discuss and provide feedback on risk responses.

- **One-on-One Discussions**: Have individual conversations, especially with key stakeholders, to gather more in-depth feedback.

4. Incorporate Feedback into Regular Updates

- **Feedback Loop**: Create a feedback loop where stakeholder input is regularly reviewed and used to update risk response plans.

- **Transparency**: Communicate back to stakeholders how their feedback is being used to improve risk management.

5. Encourage Open and Honest Communication

- **Safe Environment**: Foster a safe environment where stakeholders feel comfortable sharing honest feedback without fear of criticism.

- **Constructive Approach**: Encourage constructive feedback, focusing on both the strengths and areas for improvement in risk response strategies.

6. Acknowledge and Act on Feedback

- **Recognition**: Acknowledge the contributions of stakeholders in providing feedback.

- **Responsive Actions**: Demonstrate that the feedback is valued by taking concrete actions to address the comments and suggestions received.

7. Document Feedback and Actions Taken

- **Record Keeping**: Keep a record of the feedback received and the actions taken in response. This documentation can be valuable for future reference and for lessons learned sessions.

8. Follow-Up

- **Review Effectiveness**: Periodically review the effectiveness of the implemented changes based on the feedback.

- **Continuous Engagement**: Keep stakeholders engaged in the risk management process, updating them on changes and seeking ongoing input.

Conclusion

Encouraging and utilizing stakeholder feedback in risk response is vital for adaptive and effective risk management. It helps in ensuring that risk responses are aligned with project needs and stakeholder expectations. Creating an open, communicative environment and showing responsiveness to feedback are key to fostering stakeholder engagement and continuous improvement in risk management strategies.

EVALUATION AND MANAGEMENT OF SECONDARY AND RESIDUAL RISKS POST-RESPONSE IMPLEMENTATION

Evaluating and reacting to secondary and residual risks resulting from response implementation is an essential aspect of dynamic risk management. Secondary risks are those that arise as a direct result of implementing a risk response, while residual risks are those that remain after the risk responses have been executed. Here's how to approach this:

1. Identify Secondary and Residual Risks

- **Secondary Risk Identification**: After implementing a risk response, identify any new risks that have emerged as a consequence of that response.

- **Residual Risk Assessment**: Assess the risks that remain even after the risk responses have been executed. These are the risks that the responses didn't fully mitigate.

2. Evaluate the Impact and Probability

- **Impact Analysis**: Evaluate the potential impact of secondary and residual risks on the project's objectives, considering aspects like scope, schedule, cost, and quality.

- **Probability Assessment**: Assess the likelihood of each secondary and residual risk materializing.

3. Prioritize These Risks

- **Risk Prioritization**: Prioritize secondary and residual risks based on their assessed impact and probability. Focus on those that pose the greatest threat to the project's success.

4. Develop and Implement Response Plans

- **Response Strategy Development**: For high-priority secondary and residual risks, develop appropriate response strategies. These could include mitigation, transfer, acceptance, or further contingency planning.

- **Implementation**: Implement these response plans, ensuring they are integrated into the overall project plan.

5. Continuous Monitoring

- **Ongoing Risk Monitoring**: Continuously monitor secondary and residual risks as the project progresses. This includes tracking any changes in their impact or probability.

- **Adjustment of Response Plans**: Be prepared to adjust risk response strategies as necessary, based on the ongoing monitoring and evaluation.

6. Stakeholder Communication

- **Inform Stakeholders**: Communicate about secondary and residual risks and the response strategies to all relevant stakeholders.

- **Feedback Loop**: Encourage stakeholders to provide feedback on the risk responses and any observed secondary or residual risks.

7. Document Changes and Actions

- **Risk Register Update**: Update the risk register to include any identified secondary and residual risks along with their response strategies.

- **Documentation of Actions**: Keep a record of all actions taken to manage these risks, including the rationale behind each decision.

8. Improvise as Needed

- **Adaptive Management**: Be flexible and ready to improvise new strategies if the situation demands, especially if the secondary or residual risks evolve unexpectedly.

- **Creative Solutions**: Encourage the team to think creatively in developing effective ways to handle these risks.

Conclusion

Evaluating and reacting to secondary and residual risks require a proactive and flexible approach to risk management. Regular identification, assessment, prioritization, and response to these risks are crucial for maintaining control over the project's risk landscape. Continuous monitoring, stakeholder engagement, and adaptability in response strategies are key to effectively managing these risks throughout the project lifecycle.

CASE STUDY: INTERNATIONAL E-COMMERCE PLATFORM LAUNCH

Context

A global retail company is launching a new e-commerce platform to expand its international online presence. The project involves significant technological, market, and operational risks. Implementing the risk response plan effectively is crucial for the successful launch and operation of the platform.

Executing the Risk Response Plan

- **Action Initiation:** Activating the predefined risk response actions as per the project's risk management plan.

- **Monitoring Progress:** Regularly tracking the progress and effectiveness of these actions against the set timelines and objectives.

Executing the Contingency Plans

- **Contingency Activation:** Implementing contingency plans for risks that materialize, such as technical failures or supply chain disruptions.

- **Adaptability:** Being prepared to modify contingency plans based on the evolving project environment and emerging challenges.

Encouraging Stakeholder Feedback

- **Feedback Mechanisms:** Establishing channels for stakeholders to provide feedback on the risk responses, such as surveys, meetings, or direct communication lines.

- **Stakeholder Engagement:** Actively involving stakeholders in reviewing and providing input on the effectiveness of risk responses.

Evaluating and Reacting to Secondary and Residual Risks

- **Secondary Risk Assessment:** Identifying and evaluating new risks that arise as a result of implementing the risk responses.

- **Residual Risk Monitoring:** Continuously monitoring for any residual risks that remain after risk responses have been implemented.

- **Improvisation:** Being ready to improvise and adapt the risk management approach as necessary, based on the evaluation of secondary and residual risks.

Conclusion

In the context of the international e-commerce platform launch, implementing the risk response plan involves executing predefined actions, activating contingency plans, and actively engaging stakeholders for feedback. The project risk manager must be vigilant in monitoring the effectiveness of these responses and be prepared to address secondary and residual risks. This approach ensures that the project remains resilient and adaptable to changes, aligning with the dynamic nature of global e-commerce projects. By continuously evaluating and reacting to the risk landscape, the project team can better navigate the complexities of launching and operating an international e-commerce platform, thereby enhancing the likelihood of its success.

DOMAIN V
MONITOR AND CLOSE RISKS

Task 1 Gather and analyze performance data

RECONCILIATION OF PERFORMANCE DATA AND REPORTS FROM RISK-RELEVANT WORK PACKAGES

Reconciling performance data and reports from risk-relevant work packages is a crucial task in Domain V of risk management, which involves monitoring and closing risks. This process ensures that the data regarding the execution of work packages, especially those impacted by identified risks, aligns with the overall project performance and risk management plans. Here's how to approach this task:

1. Gather Performance Data and Reports

- **Collect Data**: Start by collecting all performance data and reports related to work packages, especially those identified as being high risk or having significant risk exposure.

- **Risk-Relevant Information**: Focus on data that directly relates to risk management efforts, such as mitigation actions, response strategies, and outcomes.

Alexander Stratton

2. Review Work Package Deliverables

- **Deliverable Check**: Assess the deliverables of each work package against its objectives and requirements. Ensure that the deliverables meet the expected standards and project specifications.

- **Timeline Review**: Review the completion timelines of the work packages against the planned schedule, noting any delays or accelerations.

3. Compare Against Risk Management Plan

- **Alignment with Risk Responses**: Compare the actual performance of the work packages with the planned risk responses. Check if the risk mitigation or contingency plans were executed as intended and if they were effective.

- **Variance Identification**: Identify any variances between the planned and actual risk responses, and understand the reasons behind these variances.

4. Analyze Performance Metrics

- **Key Performance Indicators (KPIs)**: Analyze the key performance indicators relevant to each work package. This might include metrics like cost performance, schedule adherence, quality metrics, and resource utilization.

- **Metric Comparison**: Compare these metrics against the baseline measurements established at the project's outset or at the time of risk identification.

5. Document Findings

- **Record Discrepancies**: Document any discrepancies, variances, or noteworthy findings in the performance of the work packages, especially as they relate to risk management.

- **Update Risk Register**: Update the risk register with the latest information regarding the execution of risk responses in these work packages.

6. Communicate with Relevant Stakeholders

- **Report to Stakeholders**: Prepare and communicate reports to relevant stakeholders, summarizing the findings from the reconciliation of performance data.

- **Feedback Loop**: Encourage feedback from stakeholders on the findings and any further insights they might offer.

7. Use Findings for Continuous Improvement

- **Lessons Learned**: Use the insights gained from reconciling performance data to refine future risk response strategies and work package management.

- **Adjust Risk Management Plan**: Adjust the overall risk management plan as necessary based on the findings.

Conclusion

Reconciling performance data and reports from risk-relevant work packages is essential for ensuring that risk management strategies are effectively implemented and integrated into the overall project management. This process involves a detailed review of deliverables, timelines, and performance metrics, and necessitates clear documentation and communication with stakeholders. The insights gained from this reconciliation are invaluable for continuous improvement in risk management practices.

DATA ANALYSIS TO ASCERTAIN PROJECT COMPLETION STATUS AGAINST BASELINE

Analyzing data to determine the completion status of a project against the baseline involves a systematic comparison of current project performance with the planned or baseline metrics. This analysis helps in identifying any deviations from the plan and understanding the progress of the project. Here's how to approach this task:

1. Gather Current Project Data

- **Collect Data**: Compile current data related to project deliverables, schedule, budget, resource usage, and quality metrics.

- **Data Sources**: Include data from progress reports, work package updates, financial reports, and performance metrics.

2. Review Project Baseline

- **Baseline Metrics**: Revisit the project baseline, which includes the original scope, schedule, cost, resource allocation, and quality expectations set at the project's outset.

- **Documentation**: Ensure that the baseline documentation is up-to-date and accurately reflects what was initially planned.

3. Compare Current Data with Baseline

- **Schedule Comparison**: Compare the current project timeline with the baseline schedule. Identify any areas where the project is ahead, on track, or behind schedule.

- **Budget Analysis**: Assess how the actual spending compares to the budgeted amounts. Note any variances in cost expenditure.

- **Scope Assessment**: Evaluate if the project deliverables completed so far align with the planned scope. Check for any scope creep or changes.

- **Resource Utilization**: Analyze the usage of resources against what was planned. Identify overuse or underutilization of resources.

- **Quality Metrics**: Compare current quality metrics with the baseline standards to assess if the project deliverables meet the expected quality.

4. Identify Variances and Reasons

- **Variance Identification**: Document variances between the current project status and the baseline in terms of schedule, cost, scope, resources, and quality.

- **Root Cause Analysis**: Conduct a root cause analysis to understand why these variances occurred.

5. Document and Report Findings

- **Update Status Reports**: Document the findings in a status report, detailing how the project is performing against each baseline metric.

- **Visual Representations**: Use charts, graphs, and tables to visually represent the data, making the comparison more accessible and understandable.

6. Communicate with Stakeholders

- **Stakeholder Briefing**: Present the findings to project stakeholders, including project sponsors, team members, and other relevant parties.

- **Feedback Mechanism**: Encourage stakeholders to provide feedback or insights that might explain variances or contribute to adjustments.

7. Plan Adjustments if Necessary

- **Action Plans**: If significant variances are identified, develop action plans to bring the project back on track or to adjust the baseline to reflect the current reality.

- **Stakeholder Approval**: Obtain approvals for any changes or adjustments from necessary stakeholders.

Conclusion

Analyzing project data to determine the completion status against the baseline is vital for effective project control and management. It provides a clear picture of the project's progress and highlights areas needing attention or adjustment. Regular and systematic comparison, thorough documentation, and clear communication with stakeholders are key to this process, ensuring that the project remains aligned with its objectives and can adapt to changing circumstances.

EXECUTION OF VARIANCE ANALYSIS

Performing a variance analysis in project management involves comparing actual project performance against the planned or baseline performance. This analysis helps identify differences (variances) between what was planned and what has been achieved, providing insights into areas that may need attention or adjustment. Here's how to conduct a variance analysis:

1. Gather Actual and Planned Data

- **Collect Data**: Obtain actual project data such as costs incurred, time spent, resources used, and progress made on deliverables.

- **Baseline Data**: Retrieve the planned or baseline data for these same aspects (costs, schedule, resources, scope) from the project management plan.

2. Calculate Variances

- **Cost Variance**: Calculate the difference between the actual costs and the budgeted costs.
  CostVariance(CV)=BudgetedCostofWorkPerformed(BCWP)−ActualCostofWorkPerformed(ACWP)

- **Schedule Variance**: Assess the difference between the actual progress and the planned progress.

ScheduleVariance(SV)=BudgetedCostofWorkPerformed(BCWP)–Budge
tedCostofWorkScheduled(BCWS)

- **Scope and Quality Variances**: Evaluate any deviations in scope and quality from the baseline. This could include changes in deliverables, specifications, or quality metrics.

3. Analyze the Reasons for Variances

- **Investigate Causes**: For each variance identified, investigate the underlying reasons. This could involve factors like changes in project scope, unforeseen challenges, resource availability issues, or estimation inaccuracies.

- **Stakeholder Input**: Engage with project team members and stakeholders to get their insights into why variances have occurred.

4. Evaluate Impact

- **Impact on Project Objectives**: Assess the impact of these variances on overall project objectives, including the potential effects on project completion, costs, and quality.

- **Future Implications**: Consider how these variances might affect the future course of the project.

5. Report Findings

- **Document Findings**: Prepare a variance analysis report that documents the variances, their causes, and their impacts.

- **Visual Tools**: Use charts and graphs to visually represent the variances, making the information more accessible.

6. Communicate with Stakeholders

- **Share with Stakeholders**: Present the variance analysis findings to project stakeholders, including sponsors, team members, and clients.

- **Feedback and Discussion**: Encourage discussion and feedback on the findings to gain additional insights and perspectives.

7. Develop Response Strategies

- **Corrective Actions**: Based on the variance analysis, develop corrective actions to address negative variances and bring the project back on track.

- **Adjust Project Plan**: If necessary, adjust the project plan to reflect the new reality and re-baseline as appropriate.

8. Monitor Ongoing Performance

- **Continuous Monitoring**: Continue to monitor project performance against the adjusted plan.

- **Regular Variance Analysis**: Conduct regular variance analyses to ensure the project remains aligned with its objectives and to identify any new variances as they occur.

Conclusion

Variance analysis is a critical tool in project management for monitoring project performance and ensuring that the project remains aligned with its objectives. It involves a systematic comparison of actual performance against planned performance, understanding the causes of variances, and taking appropriate corrective actions. Effective communication, documentation, and stakeholder engagement are key to the success of this process.

MONITORING PROJECT RISK IMPACT ON OVERALL ENTERPRISE RISK EXPOSURE

Monitoring the impact of project risks on the overall risk exposure of an enterprise is a crucial aspect of comprehensive risk management. This process involves assessing how individual project risks might affect the broader organizational risk profile. Here's a structured approach to conducting this monitoring:

1. Understand Organizational Risk Profile

- **Baseline Risk Exposure**: Start with a clear understanding of the organization's baseline risk exposure. This includes risks across all areas of the enterprise, not just those specific to the project.

- **Enterprise Risk Management (ERM) Framework**: Review the organization's ERM framework to understand how project risks fit within the broader risk context.

2. Aggregate Project Risks

- **Compilation of Project Risks**: Compile all identified risks from the project, including both current and potential future risks.

- **Assess Cumulative Impact**: Assess the cumulative impact of these risks on the project, considering factors like likelihood, severity, and interdependencies.

3. Analyze Impact on Organizational Risk

- **Cross-Project Analysis**: Analyze how the risks from the project interact with risks from other projects or operational areas of the enterprise.

- **Overall Risk Exposure**: Assess how the aggregated project risks might alter the organization's overall risk exposure. Consider both quantitative and qualitative impacts.

4. Monitor Key Risk Indicators (KRIs)

- **Identify KRIs**: Identify Key Risk Indicators relevant to both the project and the organization. KRIs are metrics used to provide an early signal of increasing risk exposure.

- **Continuous Monitoring**: Set up a system for continuous monitoring of these KRIs to quickly detect changes in risk exposure.

5. Integrate with Organizational Risk Management

- **Alignment with ERM**: Ensure that project risk monitoring is integrated with the organization's ERM processes. This includes alignment in risk assessment methodologies and reporting structures.

- **Feedback Loop**: Create a feedback loop between the project risk management and the organizational ERM function.

6. Report and Communicate

- **Regular Reporting**: Provide regular reports to organizational stakeholders, including risk managers and executive leadership, on the project's impact on overall risk exposure.

- **Clear Communication**: Communicate in clear, non-technical language the implications of the project risks on the broader organizational risk profile.

7. Adjust Risk Responses

- **Organizational Risk Strategy**: Adjust risk responses at the project level in alignment with the organization's overall risk strategy and tolerance levels.

- **Dynamic Response Planning**: Be prepared to dynamically adjust risk response plans as the project progresses and as its impact on organizational risk exposure evolves.

8. Document and Learn

- **Lessons Learned**: Document lessons learned from the process of monitoring and managing the project's impact on organizational risk exposure.

- **Continuous Improvement**: Use these insights for continuous improvement in both project and enterprise risk management practices.

Conclusion

Monitoring the impact of project risks on overall organizational risk exposure is key for ensuring that risks at the project level are managed in line with the broader risk management objectives of the enterprise. This process requires continuous assessment, integration with enterprise risk management frameworks, and effective communication with organizational stakeholders. Regular adjustments and dynamic response planning are essential to manage the evolving risk landscape effectively.

CASE STUDY: EXPANSION OF A TELECOMMUNICATIONS NETWORK

Context

A telecommunications company is expanding its network infrastructure to provide enhanced services in underserved areas. This project involves significant technical, logistical, and regulatory risks. Gathering and analyzing performance data is critical to ensure the project stays on track and within the defined risk parameters.

Reconciling Performance Data from Risk-Relevant Work Packages

- **Data Collection:** Gathering performance data from various work packages, such as network installation, regulatory compliance, and community engagement.

- **Reconciliation:** Comparing the collected data against the risk management plan to identify any discrepancies or anomalies.

Analyzing Data to Determine Completion Status Against Baseline

- **Baseline Comparison**: Evaluating the progress of work packages against the planned timeline, budget, and quality standards.

- **Status Reporting:** Documenting the completion status of each work package, highlighting any areas that are ahead, on track, or behind schedule.

Performing Variance Analysis

- **Identifying Variances:** Calculating the variance between actual performance and the project baseline in terms of cost, time, and scope.

- **Root Cause Analysis:** Investigating the causes of significant variances to understand underlying issues and inform corrective actions.

Monitoring Impact Against Overall Project Risk Exposure

- **Risk Exposure Assessment:** Assessing how performance variances impact the overall risk exposure of the project.

- **Enterprise Impact Analysis:** Considering the implications of the project's risk exposure on the broader enterprise, such as reputational risk, financial impact, and strategic objectives.

- **Adjustment Recommendations:** Suggesting adjustments to the risk management plan based on the current risk exposure and performance data.

Conclusion

In the telecommunications network expansion project, gathering and analyzing performance data is a crucial aspect of risk management. Reconciling data from risk-relevant work packages and analyzing it against the baseline helps to track progress and identify areas requiring attention. Performing variance analysis provides insights into the causes of deviations from the plan. Monitoring the impact of these variances on the overall project risk exposure and the broader enterprise is essential for making informed decisions and adjustments to the risk management strategy. This approach aligns with PMI standards and ensures that the project adapts effectively to changing conditions and maintains alignment with the organization's strategic goals.

Task 2 Monitor residual & secondary risks

ONGOING MONITORING OF RISK RESPONSES AND DOCUMENTATION OF RESIDUAL RISKS

Monitoring risk response and documenting residual risk is an integral part of effective risk management in a project. Residual risks are those that remain after risk response strategies have been implemented. Here's how to approach this task:

1. Continuous Monitoring of Risk Responses

- **Track Implementation**: Regularly monitor the implementation of risk response actions to ensure they are being executed as planned.

- **Effectiveness Assessment**: Assess the effectiveness of these responses in reducing or managing the risks.

2. Identify and Assess Residual Risks

- **Identification**: After risk responses are implemented, identify any remaining risks. These are the residual risks, which are not completely eliminated by the response strategies.

- **Severity Assessment**: Evaluate the severity and likelihood of these residual risks. Determine if they are within acceptable limits as defined by the project's risk tolerance.

3. Document Residual Risks

- **Risk Register Update**: Update the project's risk register to include all identified residual risks, along with their updated assessments in terms of impact and probability.

- **Detailed Descriptions**: Provide detailed descriptions of each residual risk, including how they might affect the project if they materialize.

4. Review and Update Risk Response Plans

- **Adjustments to Plans**: If any residual risks are higher than acceptable levels, review and adjust the risk response plans to further mitigate these risks.

- **Alternative Strategies**: Consider alternative risk response strategies if current actions are not effectively reducing the risk to an acceptable level.

5. Communication with Stakeholders

- **Inform Stakeholders**: Regularly communicate with stakeholders about the status of residual risks and the effectiveness of response strategies.

- **Feedback Mechanism**: Encourage stakeholders to provide feedback and input on the handling of residual risks.

6. Regular Reporting

- **Reporting Schedule**: Establish a regular schedule for reporting on residual risks, such as in routine project status meetings or reports.

- **Visual Tools**: Utilize visual tools like charts or graphs in reports to clearly convey the status and impact of residual risks.

7. Integration with Project Planning

- **Alignment with Project Plans**: Ensure that the management of residual risks is integrated into the overall project planning and execution processes.

- **Contingency Plans**: Update or develop contingency plans for residual risks that might have significant impacts.

Conclusion

Monitoring risk response and documenting residual risk are critical for understanding and managing the ongoing risks in a project. It involves continuous tracking, assessment, and communication of the effectiveness of risk responses and the status of residual risks. Regular updates to the risk register and risk response plans, combined with transparent communication with stakeholders, are essential for effective residual risk management.

CONTINUOUS MONITORING OF RISK RESPONSES FOR SECONDARY RISKS

Monitoring risk response for secondary risks involves tracking and managing the risks that arise as a direct result of implementing primary risk responses. These secondary risks may not have been part of the original risk analysis but can significantly impact the project if not managed effectively. Here's a structured approach to monitor these risks:

1. Identification of Secondary Risks

- **Risk Response Review**: Review the implemented risk responses to identify potential secondary risks. These are new risks that have emerged as a consequence of the actions taken to manage primary risks.

- **Stakeholder Input**: Engage with project team members and stakeholders to gather their insights and observations on any emerging secondary risks.

2. Assess Secondary Risks

- **Impact and Probability Assessment**: Evaluate the impact and likelihood of each identified secondary risk. Determine how these risks might affect the project's objectives.

- **Prioritization**: Prioritize secondary risks based on their assessed severity and probability, focusing on those that pose the greatest threat to the project.

3. Document Secondary Risks

- **Risk Register Update**: Update the project's risk register to include all identified secondary risks, along with their assessments and potential impact on the project.

- **Detailed Documentation**: Provide clear descriptions of each secondary risk, including possible triggers, impacts, and recommended response strategies.

4. Develop and Implement Response Strategies

- **Response Planning**: Develop appropriate response strategies for the most significant secondary risks. Strategies could include mitigation, transfer, acceptance, or further contingency planning.

- **Integration with Project Plan**: Ensure that these risk response strategies are integrated into the overall project plan.

5. Continuous Monitoring

- **Regular Tracking**: Establish a process for the continuous monitoring of secondary risks. This includes tracking any changes in their status or impact.

- **Dynamic Management**: Be prepared to adjust risk response strategies for secondary risks as the project progresses and as new information becomes available.

6. Communication with Stakeholders

- **Regular Updates**: Provide regular updates to stakeholders on the status of secondary risks and the effectiveness of response strategies.

- **Feedback and Adaptation**: Encourage feedback from stakeholders and adapt your risk management approaches based on this input.

7. Review and Adjustments

- **Periodic Review**: Periodically review the management of secondary risks to evaluate the effectiveness of response strategies and to identify any new secondary risks.

- **Plan Adjustments**: Adjust the project plan and risk response strategies as necessary to address the evolving risk landscape.

Conclusion

Monitoring risk response for secondary risks is a crucial part of dynamic risk management. It requires vigilance in identifying new risks arising from initial risk responses, continuous assessment and prioritization, effective documentation, and ongoing communication with stakeholders. Regular review and adjustment of response strategies are key to ensuring these risks are managed proactively and do not adversely impact the project's success.

EVALUATION OF THE IMPACT OF RESIDUAL AND SECONDARY RISKS ON PROJECT OBJECTIVES

Assessing the impact of residual and secondary risks on project objectives involves a thorough evaluation of how these remaining or newly emerged risks could affect the project's scope, schedule, budget, quality, and overall success. Here's a structured approach to conduct this assessment:

1. Understand Project Objectives

- **Objective Review**: Begin by clearly understanding the project's key objectives, including scope, time, cost, quality, and any specific stakeholder expectations.

- **Baseline for Assessment**: Use these objectives as a baseline to assess the impact of risks.

2. Identify and Prioritize Residual and Secondary Risks

- **Risk Identification**: Identify all residual risks (risks that remain after initial mitigation efforts) and secondary risks (new risks arising from the implementation of risk responses).

- **Risk Prioritization**: Prioritize these risks based on their potential impact and probability of occurrence.

3. Evaluate Impact on Project Objectives

- **Scope Impact**: Assess how these risks might change the project's scope. Consider both expansions (scope creep) and reductions.

- **Schedule Impact**: Evaluate the potential for these risks to delay project milestones or necessitate changes in the project timeline.

- **Cost Impact**: Determine how residual and secondary risks might lead to cost overruns or require additional budget allocation.

- **Quality Impact**: Consider the effect of these risks on the project's quality standards and deliverables.

- **Stakeholder Impact**: Assess how these risks might affect stakeholder satisfaction and the project's ability to meet its commitments.

4. Quantitative and Qualitative Analysis

- **Quantitative Analysis**: Where possible, use quantitative methods (like expected monetary value analysis) to assess the potential financial impact of risks.

- **Qualitative Analysis**: Use qualitative analysis to understand the non-quantifiable impacts, such as on team morale or client trust.

5. Document the Assessment

- **Risk Register Update**: Document the findings of the impact assessment in the risk register, detailing how each residual and secondary risk can impact the project objectives.

- **Impact Descriptions**: Provide detailed descriptions of the potential impact, including best-case and worst-case scenarios.

6. Communicate with Stakeholders

- **Stakeholder Briefing**: Communicate the outcomes of the impact assessment to project stakeholders. Include how these risks could potentially derail or alter project objectives.

- **Feedback Mechanism**: Encourage stakeholders to provide feedback or additional insights on the risk impact assessment.

7. Develop Impact Mitigation Strategies

- **Response Strategies**: Develop strategies to mitigate the impact of these risks on project objectives. This might include additional mitigation actions, contingency plans, or acceptance with close monitoring.

- **Integration into Project Plan**: Ensure these strategies are integrated into the overall project management plan.

Conclusion

Assessing the impact of residual and secondary risks on project objectives is critical for maintaining control over the project's trajectory and ensuring its success. This process requires a detailed understanding of both the risks and the project objectives, as well as regular communication with stakeholders. Effective documentation and ongoing monitoring are essential to manage these risks proactively and ensure they do not adversely affect the project's outcomes.

UPDATING AND COMMUNICATING THE IMPACT OF RESIDUAL AND SECONDARY RISKS

Updating and communicating the impact of residual and secondary risks is a vital aspect of ongoing risk management in a project. This process involves regularly revising the risk assessment to reflect any changes in these risks and ensuring that all stakeholders are informed about their potential impact. Here's a structured approach to this task:

1. Regularly Update Risk Assessments

- **Review Residual and Secondary Risks**: Periodically review and update the assessments of residual and secondary risks. This includes re-evaluating their probability, impact, and potential effect on project objectives.

- **Document Changes**: Record any changes in the risk status, including new developments or changes in the project environment that affect these risks.

2. Revise Risk Response Strategies

- **Adjustment of Strategies**: Based on the updated assessments, adjust the risk response strategies for residual and secondary risks. This may include developing new mitigation strategies or modifying existing ones.

- **Resource Allocation**: Ensure that resources are appropriately allocated for the updated risk responses.

3. Maintain an Updated Risk Register

- **Risk Register Revision**: Continuously update the risk register with the latest information on residual and secondary risks, including their updated assessments and response plans.

- **Clear Documentation**: Ensure that the risk register provides clear, detailed descriptions of each risk and its potential impacts.

4. Communicate with Stakeholders

- **Regular Reports**: Prepare regular reports summarizing the status and impact of residual and secondary risks. Include any changes in risk status or response strategies.

- **Stakeholder Meetings**: Use regular project meetings or specific risk review meetings to discuss these risks and their impacts with stakeholders.

- **Tailored Communication**: Customize the information and its presentation according to the needs and interests of different stakeholder groups.

5. Incorporate Feedback

- **Seek Stakeholder Input**: Actively seek feedback from stakeholders on the risk management process, particularly regarding residual and secondary risks.

- **Feedback Incorporation**: Incorporate this feedback into the ongoing risk management process.

6. Use Visual Tools for Communication

- **Charts and Graphs**: Utilize visual tools like charts, graphs, and heat maps to convey the status and impact of these risks effectively.

- **Clarity and Accessibility**: Ensure that these visual representations are clear and easily understandable to all stakeholders.

7. Plan for Regular Updates

- **Scheduled Reviews**: Establish a schedule for regular review and update sessions for residual and secondary risks.

- **Adaptability**: Be prepared to conduct unscheduled reviews in response to significant project changes or external events.

Conclusion

Effectively updating and communicating the impact of residual and secondary risks is essential for maintaining transparency and ensuring that all project stakeholders are aligned in understanding and managing these risks. Regular updates, clear documentation, tailored communication, and stakeholder engagement are key to this process, ensuring that the project can adapt to and effectively manage ongoing and emerging risks.

CASE STUDY: CONSTRUCTION OF A LARGE-SCALE GREEN ENERGY PLANT

Context

A major energy company is constructing a large-scale green energy plant. This project is complex and subject to various risks, including environmental, technical, and regulatory challenges. Monitoring residual and secondary risks is critical to ensure project success and alignment with sustainability goals.

Monitoring Risk Response and Documenting Residual Risk

- **Continuous Monitoring:** Regularly tracking the effectiveness of risk responses implemented throughout the project.

- **Residual Risk Documentation:** Identifying and documenting any residual risks that remain after risk responses have been executed. For example, documenting remaining environmental impact risks despite mitigation strategies.

Monitoring Risk Response for Secondary Risks

- **Secondary Risk Identification:** Watching for new risks that arise as a direct consequence of implementing risk responses. For instance, identifying community relations risks that may emerge from environmental mitigation measures.

- **Impact Assessment:** Evaluating the potential impact of these secondary risks on the project.

Assessing Impact of Residual and Secondary Risks on Project Objectives

- **Objective Alignment:** Assessing how residual and secondary risks might affect key project objectives, such as sustainability targets, budget, timeline, and stakeholder expectations.

- **Risk Re-evaluation:** Continuously re-evaluating these risks to determine if further action or adjustment to the risk management plan is needed.

Updating and Communicating Impact of Residual and Secondary Risks

- **Regular Updates:** Providing updated information on the status and impact of residual and secondary risks to all relevant stakeholders.

- **Communication Channels:** Using established communication channels such as regular meetings, reports, and digital platforms to disseminate updates.

- **Stakeholder Engagement:** Actively engaging stakeholders in discussions about the impact of these risks and potential strategies for further mitigation or adaptation.

Conclusion

In the context of the green energy plant construction project, monitoring residual and secondary risks is a dynamic and ongoing process. By continuously tracking the effectiveness of risk responses and documenting any remaining or new risks, the project risk manager can ensure that the project remains aligned with its objectives and responds adaptively to changing risk conditions. Regular assessment and communication of the impact of these risks are crucial to keep stakeholders informed and engaged. This approach is in line with PMI standards for effective risk management and is critical to the success and sustainability of complex construction projects in the energy sector.

Task 3 Provide information required to update relevant project documents

AGGREGATING, SUMMARIZING, AND UPDATING PROJECT DOCUMENTS WITH RISK DATA

Aggregating and summarizing risk data to update project documents is a critical task in effective risk management. This process involves collecting all risk-related information, analyzing it for insights, and then updating various project documents to reflect the current risk landscape. Here's how to approach this task:

1. Aggregate Risk Data

- **Collect Data**: Gather all risk-related data from various sources within the project, including risk assessments, risk registers, meeting minutes, and reports.

- **Comprehensive Coverage**: Ensure the data covers all aspects of risk management, including identified risks, risk responses, outcomes of risk treatment, and any newly identified risks.

2. Summarize Key Findings

- **Risk Analysis**: Analyze the aggregated data to identify key trends, patterns, and insights. Focus on the effectiveness of risk responses, emerging risk trends, and areas of successful risk mitigation.

- **Summary Report**: Create a summary report highlighting these key findings, including any significant changes in risk status.

3. Update the Risk Register

- **Risk Register Revision**: Update the risk register with the latest information. This includes adding new risks, adjusting the probability and impact of existing risks, and documenting the outcomes of risk responses.

- **Current Status**: Ensure that the risk register accurately reflects the current risk status of the project.

4. Update Lessons Learned

- **Document Lessons**: Update the project's lessons learned document with new insights gained from recent risk management activities. Include what worked well, what didn't, and why.

- **Best Practices**: Highlight any best practices or strategies that proved effective in managing risks.

5. Revise the Project Management Plan

- **Plan Adjustments**: Make necessary adjustments to the project management plan to account for the updated risk information. This may include changes in project approaches, timelines, or resource allocations.

- **Alignment**: Ensure that the project management plan aligns with the current risk landscape and mitigation strategies.

6. Update Change Logs

- **Record Changes**: Update the change logs to include any changes made to the project as a result of risk management activities. This includes changes in scope, schedule, budget, or quality specifications.

- **Traceability**: Maintain traceability between changes and the corresponding risks that triggered them.

7. Communication and Distribution

- **Stakeholder Communication**: Communicate the updates in risk data and the corresponding changes in project documents to all relevant stakeholders.

- **Accessibility**: Ensure that updated documents are accessible to all project team members and stakeholders who need them.

8. Continuous Monitoring and Updating

- **Regular Reviews**: Establish a regular schedule for reviewing and updating risk data and project documents.

- **Dynamic Process**: Treat risk data aggregation and documentation as a dynamic process, adapting to changes in the project environment.

Conclusion

Aggregating and summarizing risk data for the update of project documents ensures that all relevant information is captured, analyzed, and reflected in key project management tools. This process is crucial for maintaining an accurate and up-to-date view of the project's risk landscape, informing decision-making, and guiding ongoing project management efforts. Regular communication and engagement with stakeholders are essential to ensure transparency and alignment in risk management practices.

MONITORING AND CLOSING EXPIRED RISKS

Monitoring and closing out expired risks is an important aspect of risk management, ensuring that the focus remains on current and relevant risks. Expired risks are those that are no longer a concern due to changes in project conditions, completion of certain project phases, or successful mitigation. Here's a structured approach to this process:

1. Regular Review of Risk Register

- **Scheduled Reviews**: Conduct regular reviews of the risk register to assess the status of each listed risk.

- **Identify Changes**: Look for risks that may no longer be relevant due to changes in the project's scope, timeline, or environment.

2. Assess Risk Expiry Criteria

- **Define Expiry Criteria**: Establish clear criteria for determining when a risk can be considered expired. This could include completion of a project phase, implementation of a successful mitigation strategy, or a change in external conditions rendering the risk irrelevant.

- **Evaluate Against Criteria**: Assess each risk against these criteria to determine if it has expired.

3. Consult with Project Team and Stakeholders

- **Team Input**: Engage with the project team and relevant stakeholders to get their input on the status of risks. They may provide insights on whether certain risks are still applicable or have been effectively mitigated.

- **Expert Opinion**: In some cases, seek opinions from subject matter experts, especially for complex or technical risks.

4. Documenting Risk Closure

- **Update Risk Register**: For each risk that is deemed expired, update the risk register to reflect its closure. Include a brief note on why the risk is considered expired.

- **Lessons Learned**: Document any lessons learned from managing these risks, which can be valuable for future projects.

5. Communicate Risk Closure

- **Inform Stakeholders**: Communicate the closure of risks to all relevant stakeholders, providing them with updates on the current risk landscape of the project.

- **Transparency**: Ensure transparency in the process of closing out risks, so all stakeholders understand the rationale behind these decisions.

6. Reallocate Resources if Necessary

- **Resource Adjustment**: If resources were allocated to manage these now-expired risks, reassess and reallocate them as needed to address current risks or other project needs.

- **Plan Adjustment**: Adjust the project plan and risk response strategies to reflect the updated risk profile.

7. Monitor for Re-emergence

- **Ongoing Vigilance**: Even after risks are closed out, maintain a level of vigilance in case they re-emerge. This is particularly important in dynamic project environments where conditions can change rapidly.

8. Continuously Update Risk Profile

- **Dynamic Risk Management**: Recognize that risk management is a dynamic process. Regularly update the overall risk profile of the project to reflect new and changing risks, as well as the closure of expired ones.

Conclusion

Monitoring and closing out expired risks is essential to maintaining an effective and focused risk management strategy. It involves regular review, clear criteria for risk expiry, stakeholder consultation, and thorough documentation. Communication and transparency in this process are key to ensuring that all project participants are aligned on the current risk status and that the project is prepared to address any evolving risks.

CASE STUDY: URBAN MASS TRANSIT SYSTEM UPGRADE

Context

A city is undertaking a major upgrade of its urban mass transit system, involving the introduction of new technologies, extension of routes, and improvement in services. The project is complex, involving numerous stakeholders and subject to a range of risks. Keeping project documents updated with the latest risk information is vital for effective project management and communication.

Aggregating and Summarizing Risk Data

- **Data Collection:** Gathering risk-related data from various sources, including team reports, automated monitoring systems, and stakeholder feedback.

- **Data Summarization:** Summarizing this data to provide a clear, concise overview of the current risk status.

Alexander Stratton

Updating Project Documents

- **Risk Register:** Regularly updating the risk register with new risks, changes in risk status, and the outcomes of risk responses.

- **Lessons Learned:** Documenting insights and learnings from risk management activities, which can inform future projects or later stages of the current project.

- **Project Management Plan:** Revising the project management plan to reflect any changes in risk status or risk management strategies.

- **Change Logs:** Maintaining logs of any changes made to the project as a result of risk management activities, including scope, schedule, or resource adjustments.

Monitoring and Closing Out Expired Risks

- **Risk Review:** Periodically reviewing the risk register to identify risks that are no longer relevant or have been resolved.

- **Risk Closure:** Formally closing out expired risks, documenting the outcomes and any final actions taken.

- **Communication:** Informing relevant stakeholders about the closure of risks and updating them on the current risk landscape of the project.

Conclusion

In the urban mass transit system upgrade project, providing information to update relevant project documents is a critical aspect of risk management. By aggregating and summarizing risk data, and regularly updating key documents like the risk register and project management plan, the project risk manager ensures that all stakeholders have up-to-date information on the risk status and management activities. Monitoring and closing out expired risks helps to maintain the relevance and accuracy of the risk register, contributing to effective and efficient project management. This approach aligns with PMI standards for project risk management, ensuring that the project adapts to changing risk conditions and maintains alignment with its objectives and stakeholder expectations.

Task 4 Monitor project risk levels

PROJECT RISK LEVEL ASSESSMENT

Assessing the project risk level is a crucial ongoing task in risk management, ensuring that the project's overall exposure to risks is understood and managed effectively. This assessment involves evaluating the current status of all identified risks, their potential impact, and the likelihood of occurrence. Here's a structured approach to assess the project risk level:

1. Review and Update Risk Assessments

- **Risk Register Review**: Regularly review the risk register to ensure it reflects the current status of all identified risks, including any new risks that have emerged.

- **Update Assessments**: Update the assessments of each risk's impact and probability as the project progresses and as new information becomes available.

2. Analyze Risk Data

- **Aggregate Risk Data**: Analyze data from the risk register, focusing on the severity and likelihood of risks. Pay attention to any trends or patterns that may be emerging.

- **Quantitative Analysis**: Where possible, use quantitative methods such as expected monetary value analysis or probabilistic modeling to assess the overall level of risk.

3. Evaluate Risk Interdependencies

- **Risk Interactions**: Assess how different risks may interact with each other. Some risks may have a cumulative effect, while others may negate each other.

- **Complex Risks**: Pay special attention to complex risks that might have a broader impact on the project.

4. Determine Overall Risk Level

- **Categorization**: Categorize the overall project risk level as low, moderate, or high based on the aggregated risk data and analysis.

- **Risk Thresholds**: Use predefined risk thresholds to help categorize the risk level. These thresholds should be based on the organization's risk appetite and tolerance.

5. Assess Impact on Project Objectives

- **Impact on Objectives**: Evaluate how the current risk level may impact the project's key objectives, such as scope, schedule, budget, and quality.

- **Scenario Analysis**: Consider different scenarios to understand the potential impact of the current risk level under varying conditions.

6. Document the Risk Level Assessment

- **Formal Documentation**: Document the findings of the risk level assessment in a formal report or update to the risk register.

- **Visual Representations**: Use charts, graphs, or heat maps to visually represent the risk levels for easier understanding and communication.

7. Regular Monitoring

- **Ongoing Assessment**: Continuously monitor the project risk level, recognizing that risks can evolve rapidly.

- **Adaptability**: Be prepared to adapt risk management strategies and plans based on changes in the overall risk level.

Conclusion

Assessing the project risk level is a dynamic and continuous process that requires regular review and updating of risk information. It involves a comprehensive analysis of individual risks, their interdependencies, and their collective impact on project objectives. Effective documentation and the use of visual tools can aid in accurately conveying the risk level to stakeholders, ensuring that risk management efforts are aligned with the project's needs and the organization's risk tolerance.

STAKEHOLDER-SPECIFIC RISK REPORTING

Preparing reports for different stakeholders in project risk management involves tailoring information to suit the specific needs and interests of each stakeholder group. Different stakeholders have varying concerns and levels of involvement in the project, so the reports should reflect this diversity. Here's a structured approach to preparing these reports:

1. Identify Stakeholder Groups

- **List Stakeholders**: Start by identifying the different stakeholder groups involved in the project. This can include project team members, project managers, sponsors, clients, suppliers, regulatory bodies, and others.

- **Understand Interests**: Understand the specific interests, concerns, and information needs of each group.

2. Determine Report Content

- **Relevant Information**: Tailor the content of each report to suit the interests of each stakeholder group. For example:

- **Project Team Members**: Focus on operational risks, task-related risks, and immediate risk response actions.

- **Project Managers and Sponsors**: Provide a high-level overview of overall project risk status, impacts on scope, schedule, and budget, and strategic risk response plans.

- **Clients and External Stakeholders**: Include information on risks that directly affect them, like potential delays or changes in project deliverables.

3. Format and Structure Reports

- **Clarity and Conciseness**: Ensure that reports are clear, concise, and easy to understand. Avoid technical jargon unless the stakeholders are familiar with it.

- **Visual Aids**: Use charts, graphs, and tables where appropriate to make the data more accessible and engaging.

4. Include Key Risk Information

- **Status of Risks**: Include the current status of key risks, including any new risks that have emerged.

- **Impact on Project Objectives**: Explain how risks impact the project's objectives, such as deadlines, budgets, and quality standards.

- **Risk Response Actions**: Detail the actions taken and planned for managing risks.

- **Future Outlook**: Provide an outlook on how risks may evolve and potential future concerns.

5. Review and Validation

- **Accuracy Check**: Ensure that all information is accurate and up-to-date.

- **Internal Review**: Have the reports reviewed internally before sending them to stakeholders to ensure clarity and accuracy.

6. Communicate and Follow-up

- **Distribution**: Distribute the reports to the respective stakeholders through appropriate channels (e.g., email, meetings, project management systems).

- **Feedback Loop**: Encourage feedback on the reports and be prepared to provide additional information or clarification as needed.

7. Document and Update Regularly

- **Regular Updates**: Prepare and distribute these reports at regular intervals – for instance, weekly, monthly, or at key project milestones.

- **Dynamic Updates**: Update the reports as significant changes occur in the project's risk profile.

Conclusion

Effective stakeholder reporting in project risk management requires understanding the unique needs of each stakeholder group and providing them with relevant, clear, and concise information. Regularly updated and well-structured reports, complemented by visual aids, ensure that stakeholders are kept informed and engaged, enabling better decision-making and support for the project.

EFFECTIVE COMMUNICATION OF RISK LEVELS TO KEY STAKEHOLDERS

Communicating risk levels to key stakeholders is a critical aspect of effective risk management. It involves clearly conveying the current status of project risks, their potential impact, and the actions being taken to manage them. This communication ensures that stakeholders are well-informed and can make decisions or provide support based on an accurate understanding of the risk landscape. Here's how to approach this communication:

1. Identify Key Stakeholders

- **Stakeholder Analysis**: Determine who the key stakeholders are for your project. This can include project sponsors, senior management, team members, clients, and external partners.

- **Understand Their Concerns**: Identify the specific risk-related concerns and information needs of these stakeholders.

2. Tailor the Message

- **Relevant Information**: Customize the information based on the stakeholder's role and interest. For example, senior management might be more interested in high-level risks and their impact on project objectives, while team members may need detailed information about operational risks.

- **Clarity and Conciseness**: Ensure that the communication is clear, concise, and free from unnecessary technical jargon.

3. Choose Appropriate Communication Channels

- **Formal Reports**: Use formal reports for structured and detailed risk information, especially for higher-level stakeholders.

- **Meetings and Presentations**: Conduct meetings or presentations for more interactive discussions on risk status and response strategies.

- **Emails and Newsletters**: Use emails or newsletters for regular, brief updates on risk status.

4. Highlight Key Risk Information

- **Current Risk Status**: Communicate the current status of key risks, including any new risks that have emerged.

- **Impact on Project**: Clearly convey how these risks impact the project's scope, schedule, budget, and quality.

- **Risk Response Actions**: Describe the actions being taken to manage these risks and any support needed from stakeholders.

- **Future Outlook**: Provide insights into how risks might evolve and future risk considerations.

5. Encourage Feedback and Discussion

- **Engage Stakeholders**: Encourage stakeholders to ask questions, provide feedback, and participate in discussions about the project's risks and management strategies.

- **Address Concerns**: Be prepared to address concerns or suggestions stakeholders may have regarding risk management.

6. Regular Updates

- **Consistent Communication**: Establish a regular schedule for communicating risk status to stakeholders, such as through weekly updates or at key project milestones.

- **Dynamic Communication**: Be prepared to communicate more frequently during periods of high risk or when significant changes occur.

7. Document Communication

- **Records of Communication**: Keep records of risk communications, including what was communicated and stakeholder responses. This can be important for accountability and for reviewing the effectiveness of the risk communication strategy.

Conclusion

Effectively communicating risk levels to key stakeholders is essential for maintaining transparency, building trust, and ensuring informed decision making in project management. It involves understanding stakeholders' needs, tailoring the message, choosing the right communication channels, and encouraging active engagement and feedback. Regular and clear communication is key to successful stakeholder management in the context of project risk.

CASE STUDY: INTERNATIONAL SPACE SATELLITE LAUNCH PROJECT

Context

A space agency is preparing for an international space satellite launch project. This high-profile project involves significant risks due to the complex nature of space technology, international collaboration, and immense costs. Monitoring and communicating the project risk levels are critical for ensuring stakeholder confidence and project success.

Assessing Project Risk Level

- **Risk Assessment:** Conducting a comprehensive review of the project to assess current risks. This includes evaluating the status of technical risks, financial risks, operational risks, and any external factors like regulatory changes or international political climates.

- **Risk Scoring:** Using a scoring system to quantify the level of risk in each area. This could include likelihood and impact assessments for each identified risk.

Preparing Reports for Different Stakeholders

- **Tailored Reporting:** Developing different versions of risk reports tailored to the interests and needs of various stakeholders. For example technical risk details for engineering teams, financial risks for investors and funding bodies, and overall project risks for government entities or international partners.

- **Clarity and Transparency:** Ensuring that the reports are clear and transparent, providing an accurate picture of risk levels without unnecessary technical jargon.

Communicating Risk Levels to Key Stakeholders

- **Regular Updates:** Providing regular updates to key stakeholders through established communication channels like briefings, email updates, and formal presentations.

- **Risk Communication Strategy:** Implementing a risk communication strategy that includes how and when risks will be communicated, ensuring timely and relevant information dissemination.

- **Engagement and Feedback:** Encouraging feedback from stakeholders on the risk reports and incorporating their insights into future risk assessments and reports.

Conclusion

In the international space satellite launch project, monitoring and effectively communicating project risk levels are essential for maintaining stakeholder trust and ensuring informed decision-making. By conducting thorough risk assessments, preparing tailored reports, and communicating effectively with key stakeholders, the project risk manager plays a crucial role in navigating the complexities and uncertainties of this high-stakes project. This approach aligns with PMI standards and is crucial for the successful completion of complex and high-risk projects like international space endeavors.